D0840147

Last Stanza
Poetry Journal

Issue #8:
Root, Bloom, Cultivate
Edited by Jenny Kalahar

Laura Crawford, artist

Stackfreed
Press

"When the Call Came" by Norbert Krapf first appeared in *Bittersweet Along the Expressway* (Waterline Books, 2000)

"Listening" by Robin Wright was first published in *Peacock Journal*

"Blackberry Leaves" by Stephen R. Roberts was originally published in *Orphic Lute*

"Bent Cows" by Stephen R. Roberts was originally published in *Bluestem* (renamed *Karamu)*

Root, bloom, cultivate.

My father was the vegetable farmer in our family. My mother adored her flower gardens. I've never had a garden, but once, over twenty years ago, I planted morning glory seeds at the base of the metal staircase of our fire escape, loving that they twine up every year without my having to ask for fresh purple blooms.

We've missed friends, coworkers, and club members these last couple of years. Many of us turned inward to reconnect with ourselves and our immediate pack, hoping the roots we set down in remote corners of our world will survive global turmoil so we might soon all bloom together again.

Some springs, I worry the morning glories won't return. Should I plant new seeds? I then get busy and never manage to buy seeds, subconsciously relying on my faith in nature. And then back they come—pale green tendrils and buds reaching at nothing, instinctively knowing that, eventually, they'll find something solid to hold.

We'll all get there, too.

Jenny Kalahar, editor

My mother, Mavis, with two of her granddaughters,
Emma and Dana in her garden

Mariupol

Inspired by "Young Girl with Candy" photo by Oleksii Kyrychenko

Alona sat on the charred windowsill
of her bombed-out home
gazing at the ruins of her once beautiful city.
She cradled a rifle on her lap
and sucked on a lollipop she found while
rummaging through what remained of her bedroom.
Most of it was in a heap three floors below,
mixed with the bricks of the outer wall.

A few razed blocks away, she could see
the remains of her school, reduced to rubble
despite being clearly designated as a shelter.
Alona wondered how many of her friends were buried
while huddling in fear in the basement.
She had stayed in her apartment to care
for her mother who was too sick to move.
Her father and brother had been killed
by Russian soldiers as they stood in a bread line.
Alona's last meager meal was three days ago,
and the melted snow she drank tasted gritty.
That's why she loved her lollipop.

The city was eerily quiet after a night of constant explosions.
A cease-fire had been announced to allow residents
to leave for refuge in neighboring countries.
A family friend, burdened with a bulging knapsack
on his back and an armful of belongings in a sack,
stood under Alona's perch and offered to take her with him.
Alona shook her head. "My mom can't be moved," she said.
"Your parents named you well.
Alona—strong as an oak tree," he said.
"But put away the gun—you'll just draw fire.
Besides, you're only nine. Children shouldn't play with guns."
Alona raised the rifle. "I'm not playing."

David Allen

Ukraine

A man stands alone
in front of a tank,
delaying its deadly mission
for a few minutes
as bombs rain down
on his Ukrainian town.
A rabid dictator
ordered this war
to rebuild Imperial Russia
and make him its newest Czar.

Democracies pass resolutions
to pick Russia's pockets,
each president lining up
to wear Chamberlain's old hat.
It's a repeat of when Hitler
sought to take over land
lost in the First World War.

Now a forty-mile parade of tanks
rumble toward Kyiv as the people
ironically make Molotov cocktails
to stubbornly resist.

I wonder what former
Soviet Bloc country
Putin will invade next.

David Allen

Lace Spun by a Queen

In youthful sleep, a claret-colored
umbel on meter stalk, you awaken,
transform into pale blush of dawn
till you mature and become vivid white.

Anise Swallowtail adores you,
flits and flutters about your head,
basks on your brilliant umbrella
array beneath Apollo's sun.

Your fairy seat of burgundy
attracts majestic honeybee,
a supplicant who desires
sips of your sweet nectar.

You are perch for goldfinch,
who embraces the day with soft
melodious tunes, then nibbles
your seeds of bountiful life.

Argiope, writing spider, spins a
silken web between your stalks,
a lacy display to rival your own
woven design of luminous ivory.

Fully matured, your umbel contracts,
becomes concave, a bird's nest
which dries out, detaches from stalk,
and becomes a tumbleweed for breeze.

Mary A. Couch

A Raft of Lilies

for Jim Keller

1

The late breeze makes them look
adrift among long shadows at the end
of the yard, these hybrid
Orientals, this gift from a dead friend.

Year after year, their light-
green javelin tips pierce
black earth and sprout
spiky leaves that gather
sunlight into cells that mix
colours for their lavish openings
where petals curl up and over
like shavings from a keen blade,
tiger striped: egg-yolk on blood-orange,
fuchsia splashed with milk,
dawn-pink streaking raincloud grey,
lilac in Venice rust,
or a monochrome flare spotted
with magic dust: mango
on violet, molé on songbird yellow,
midnight blue on thin gold.

2

Through the dark months,
he planted basil, sage, rosemary, and thyme
in foam cups on the windowsill,
tended their delicate leaves
until they softened the office
with fragrances of summer
while he basked like a plant
himself, battling depression,
spending hours at the rack

of lights above his desk,
eyes closed and his mind free
to dream responsibilities:

building a twenty-three-foot yawl
he would sail out of Hecla Island
and live on for months at a time,
crossing and crisscrossing
the seventh largest lake in the world,

or working with the stubborn
patience of a composer,
developing the unearthly strains
of open-throated blooms
                    that stir
and seem to whisper now
like travelers who have come a long way
across wide water without sound.

George Amabile

August Peonies

Lallygagging on bent stems, late
this year because of the snow
in May, their rag-tag magenta
cluster-heads freshen the still heat
like a rush of wind in the leaves
or the cool brush of deep-sea
crinolines as the ripple kiss
of a breeze opens their bunched petals
just enough to let them breathe
before they ease back
into light repose, poised
at the edge of time-lapse
attention, like us, who lose
momentum in the heavy air
rich with the scent of ripening
wheat that drifts in from the fields
over the slow-moving river
as the afternoon nods and lengthens
into shade, into thoughtfulness,
and the sky deploys an argosy
of softly tinted clouds, fresh
blooms without stems
that sail where we cannot
go, all the way to the edge
of everything, where daylight looks
back, once, then disappears.

George Amabile

The Peony Bush

After three-plus years, the peony bush
sprouting in the backyard
of the vacant house next door was
razed. Past three springs, the

peonies had yielded
wild delight—overblown
pink and white, petaled,
heads perspiring
dew, begging for release
from their weight, their
mass, their pungency. But

now, their truncated,
stumped, remnant stems
shiver in November snow. No

peonies next spring, just
corroded litter from illegally
parked vehicles in that
once-bloomed spot, deer
nibbling scrawny brush.

Hiromi Yoshida

A Blade of Grass Between Two City Stones

A spiked and oily chlorophyll kiss of triumph
for a natural blend of scraping feet
and gutter-rat gnawing,
rooted in hardened concrete arteries
of sensible suffocation under shadowed sun
that tears like dew or cracked asphalt
in a breakthrough of natural reflection
within a stained layer of dirt,
distinguished from filth by a spark of color
that screams at pedestrian populations
passing the chance to marvel
at this growth of feeling,
a freak in primal ecstasy
without constraints or complaints
in sensual squeezes that rise
into a paved path living memorial
to what exists beneath the foot
and above the fools,
scraping in time
to their cemetery waltz.

Mark Blickley

Potting Soil

There is no soil
in potting soil.

There is peat moss
dug from a black
and ancient Irish bog.
It might have
known the plows
of Celtic farmers.

There is tree bark
stripped from old pines
felled for lumber,
log homes,
cleared from farmland,
ground for paper pulp.

There is vermiculite,
prehistoric glass
mined from dormant
Armenian volcanos,
then heat-puffed
like Rice Krispies.

All this in service
to the short life
of a white geranium
signifying summer.

Kit Rohrbach

When the Call Came

When the call came,
I was about to cut the grass
for the first time. Wild
onion and dandelion were
sprouting across the lawn.
Sheaths of lily of the valley
bearing round green bells
were surrounding the lilac.

When the call came,
the yellow marsh marigolds
were rising like the sun
against a boulder in
the flowerbed. Bees
buzzed around bunches
of purple grape hyacinth.
The operator said, *I have
a collect call from Colombia.
Do you accept the charges?*
I replied, Y*es, I accept.*

When the call came,
the leathery leaves
of bloodroot along the ledge
of the stone wall were
wrapped around stalks
like green sheets on which
white petals lay. Beside
the fishpond, the fronds
of maidenhair fern were
unfurling in the sun.
A voice with a Spanish
accent spoke in my ear,
*This is a social worker. We
have a baby girl born eight
days ago. Will you accept her?*

When the call came,
the white blossoms
of the wild cherry at the edge
of the woods were fluttering
on black boughs. The tips
of Japanese irises were
pushing through the soil.
Specks of Bibb lettuce
lay like green confetti
on the upper level of
the rock garden. *Yes, we
accept her*, I said. *Yes*.

Norbert Krapf

Stella and the Angels

In memory of Stella Schmitt Prechtel

The only one of six left
on our mother's side, she
climbed all the way to ninety-six.
One hand folded back
upon itself from the arthritis
that pulses in my hands
and keeps my sister in bed
on her worst days.

Too frail to ride back
to southern Indiana in a car
from near Magnolia, Kentucky
for a reunion with kinfolks, she
sat outside on the summer grass
by the flowerbeds behind her retired
son's double-wide in the country
to pull weeds and deadhead
flowers. Her voice and smile
were eerily like our mother's,
now gone for fourteen years.

Stella smiled when she showed
me the porcelain angels she spent
the night with. She let me hold one,
but I knew to give it right back.
The framed photo of herself
she gave to me radiates
grace from the top of a chest
of drawers in the bedroom,
where I try my best to sleep.
Every waking day, Stella beams
at me like the morning star.

Norbert Krapf

A Flower I Once Hated

I think I am old enough to admit
there once was a flower I hated,
though at some point, I got over it.
It may be shocking that I could detest
something as beautiful as a flower.
It would be more accurate to say
it made me sick to my stomach.

Every time I saw and smelled it,
the flowers were arranged in a vase
in perfect order in the funeral home.
Everybody seemed to die in mum time.
I smelled formaldehyde and was staring
at a corpse. Little boy that I was, standing
there in my suit and tie, I did not know
what I was supposed to do or what emotion
to express. I made the sign of the cross
super fast, knelt, bowed my head,
pretended to say a prayer I didn't know.

For decades the words "mum" and the more
formal "chrysanthemum" made me smell
death and darkness, but something changed.
I got over it; now I love the bright colors,
the intensity in the fall of the tight petals,
the bunching up of dew in the crevices
so close to first frost. I love that this
flower prefigures the cold, bitter winter.

Some people are brought low
by the advent of winter, the loss
of daylight, the heaviness of the dark,
but I love the fall and then the winter,
the north wind that knifes into me
as I walk the streets in the morning.

I love the briskness of that wind, how
it braces as I inhale deeper, feel more alive.
Sometimes I wonder how many more mums
I will have the privilege of seeing bloom.

Norbert Krapf

Elderberry Recovery

After the long darkness of a head injury,
Petra returns to the elderberry hills.

She disappears around a bend in the lane
with a red and white thatched basket

she pulls and uplifts into constellations
of white flowers with five petals,

five stamens, and a fragrance
that blends dew and duff.

Under the tall trees, she selects
and harvests the richest clusters

from the bushes, then piles them
in heaps in her round basket.

She strides back with a bounce
and a smile that lights her face

as if she, too, were in blossom.
She holds the biggest cluster

up to her hair as if she were queen
of the elderberry woods and hills.

Her face relaxes, blue eyes expand.
In her kitchen, she makes a juice

with the potent white blossoms
that will ferment with a power

to heal herself and others who
drink of her ancient potion.

Norbert Krapf

A Family Meal

Mary was sobbing at the hearth
because the roast lamb was burnt
and the onions were black. The house
reeked of smoke as Joseph stomped
in the back door mumbling that someone
had used his best chisel as a screwdriver
to tighten the wobbly kitchen chairs.

Wood shavings caked around the corners
of his mouth, Jesus wailed away beneath
the table because nobody would change
the messy rags stuck to his bottom.

Over in the corner, the dog had lain
down with the cat, and the world was
all yowl and hiss, swat and scratch.

It was hard to believe that tomorrow
the air might clear, and sunlight
could settle again on the table.

                                    Norbert Krapf

Treemail

I read that Melbourne, Australia assigned emails to its trees to make it easier to report problems like broken branches. If our trees had email addresses, I'd have some things to say:

TO: TorreyPine@mycity.com:
Majestic in my neighbor's yard, your dramatic
silhouette against the sky at sunset gives grandeur
to the end of day. So tall, so huge, I look at you with
pleasure, grateful to appreciate you from a safe distance as
I am well aware of the weakness of your roots.

TO: LoquatTree@thishouse.com:
I did not give you my permission to plant yourself
in secret underneath the Canary Island Pine and load the ground
with loathsome fruit, sprout your spawn from hell
far and wide across my yard. Don't get too comfortable.

TO: WizenedLime@inmyyard.com:
I was so sorry when your partner passed away—
you must be lonely beset by snails, neglect.
Yet you survive and do your best. Thank you
for the three green fruits you managed to produce,
they were delicious. I don't blame you for the thorns.

TO: Apricot@intheback.com:
Overshadowed by a cypress, you refused to be bullied
by your bushy neighbor. This year's rains have helped you
put on a blossom necklace, promise sweet days to come. Here
is a coupon for a haircut to remove all those dead branches.

Joanne Sharp

Plant Wars

All starry-eyed, I planted narcissus bulbs
along the walkway. At winter, I waited
for their birth from bare earth.
Dainty white stars bloomed on clustered green spikes,
simple and neat, sweetly fragrant.

Meanwhile, marshaled forces
sent stealthy scouts underground
into the surrounding locale,
jumped their bed and grew a multitude.
All overwhelmed with cloying scent,
the balance of plant power was upset.

I put off my response to this aggression.
At last, late one spring, when their foliage
had dried to a stringy dishwater blonde,
I yanked up each and every one by the hair.
Polite daffodils who knew their place replaced them.

But they were not up to the challenge
of my haphazard care and gave up
in a couple of seasons. Years passed.
Then one day, I noticed a few narcissus,
survivors hiding in weeds along the alley.
I was merciful.

I looked the other way as the advance
moved forward, clump by clump,
until the formerly occupied territory
north of the driveway had been recolonized.
Now that obstacle, too, has been conquered,
the horde's campaign of conquest proceeds apace.

They leap from the ground like the skeleton army
in "Jason and the Argonauts," waving their green spears.
I am too old to fight this battle yet again.
The narcissus can contend with the new succulents
for the glorious possession of my yard.
May the best plant win.

Joanne Sharp

19

Ownership
February morning, 2021

My yard, left to its own devices
advertises "This Space Available."

Bees go about their business, tending
the bright yellow sourgrass while
hummingbirds jealously guard the airspace.
The fat Phoebe's daily surveys of the patio
reassure us that all is well.

A neighbor's grey tabby strolls our
common territory, grabs a backrub
from the sun-warmed driveway, then
checks behind a bromeliad by the front door
to see if the lizard might be home.

Down the alley, I wander to see if Babianas
are moving in yet. I notice one red geranium
has returned after a long absence to an
abandoned pot hiding in a secret corner.

Blue Sage and Pride of Madeira are busy serving
eviction notices to huge families of white narcissus
on this property owned by me, in name only.

Joanne Sharp

Thorns

In my garden bloom roses every year
with colors rich and heaven-scented,
and trees have grown to tower and shade
from seeds and seedlings I have planted,
and to their beauty through day and night
I can feel myself united.

And yet too often
I feel a turn within when
the darkening invasions
overpower and conquer me,
as if I've cultivated thorns.

Alys Caviness-Gober

Whispering Pines

Clearing brush beneath century pines,
I hear, just barely, my name,
but no one shares my yard
save towering firs and ferns,
wild raspberries, live-forevers,
and a ragged lawn invaded
by insistent creeping charlie.

I hear again a surer, distant whisper—
Mother—calling to a sundrenched child
from the house on Pine Street
through the back screen door
bordered by green ivy, humming
with shaded bees,
and, at the center, her,
calling from
that dark, mysterious interior,
the house's hungry heart.

Nancy Kay Peterson

New Born
For Owen

A released hallelujah rising to the sky,
    a newborn curls like a tree frog
        to my chest. Now is all

he knows in each virgin instant.
    Culmination, double helix braided,
        branching; almost perfect

hand. On the smallest of small fingers,
    a bump, mark of where the pattern
        almost broke into a sixth finger.

In the end, the design of seven thousand
    generations held; now fingers closed,
        knuckles pressed into heavy cheeks,

his fragile head in sleep
    posed as if assuming an attitude
        of weary wariness.

Michael Ansara

King of Pentacles, Knight of Pentacles

He and I were carved from the same stone,
dressed the same as teenagers, and listened to the same music.
My stepmother makes comments to one,
meant for both my father and me to hear.
Two halves of a whole, one is never seen without the other.
At night, faceless entities I see in the corner of my room
plague his nightmares,
and the cursed blood running through his veins
courses through my own.
Heat intolerance, migraines,
depression, addiction, rotten teeth.
Nurses ask for my family medical history, and I chuckle.
Do you want it alphabetically or by parent?
My social worker calls him,
asking if it's genetic or ....
He screams at himself in the mirror,
and I'm sure I've screamed those words before.
After another diagnosis, I call my father,
telling him I've found something to explain his muscle aches.

You know who you remind me of?
I already know the answer, but I laugh anyway.
The apple never falls far from the tree in this family.
I look around and see piles of rotten apples
sharing maggots and bacteria,
wondering if they know they're doing it to themselves
and to each other.
Break the cycle. Break the cycle. Break the cycle.
I can't break free
while my father's maggots
are still stuck to me.

Envy Cardena

The Tree

The dry tree at the front door of our house
was dying, little by little,
so my mother decided to cut it.
With the first blow of the ax,
the picture of my father planting that tree
fell to the floor.
On the second hit, the picture of my mother
in her wedding dress fell, too.
With the third,
the coffins of my brothers crashed.
On the fourth, the tree itself fell,
and we cried until morning.

Qassim Saudi
Translated by Jeffrey Clapp and Muntather Alsawad

Planting a Tree

If you were to come to me,
I would have no hesitation.
I would know what to do on
Arbor Day.

The root will take
in the soft brown mound.
I'd work the earth with my fingers,
create a moist opening just so   .
in the loamy topsoil.

I'd deliberately smooth the earth
around the root,
lift it with a heave,
ooze foam and feel satisfied
when the fertile work is done.

The earth gives to the tree,
and the tree gives back.
They long to take communion to
thank Mother for the budding sacrament.

We live each in our own woods—
I here, you in the next town.
Now, I ask, how can you turn
away from such bounty?

E. Martin Pedersen

A Peacock in Tennessee

With apologies to Wallace Stevens

Two peacocks refuse to spread their plumage for the tourists,
lounging beneath ancient trees kings and queens strolled among
behind high walls in Seville, Spain. Neither do they cry.

They are sublime like the sojourners of Georges Seurat seen
in a park from afar, arm in arm and never arriving.

I once saw a peacock perched on a roof in Knoxville, Tennessee.
He stretched his neck and spread his ornate plumage and screamed
into the sky. I could hear him through tinted glass as I drove by.

Still, I take out my camera here among tall cedars centuries old.
I walk on a gravel path in the verdure, treading ever lightly.
I focus on what I see and not what I recall. This is what we must.

David Vancil

Painting the Tin Roof

In memory of W. Bryant Bachman, friend and teacher

While it groaned in the Louisiana sun, we brushed
emerald green onto the rusting tin roof, a requirement
for the VA loan. I begged pardon for splotching a dab
on the white trim. "It doesn't matter, Dave," you said.
"Things can't be perfect. We'll leave it as a sign."

We worked our way out from the chimney toward
the edges, covering streaks of rust on rippled metal.
Above us, the sky seemed flawless. A small plane
buzzed us like a honeybee searching for nectar.

Two women pulled into your gravel driveway
to welcome you to the neighborhood. One called up
for permission to pluck the lone red rose adorning
the trellis. "Yes, ladies, please do," you answered.

We made short work of what remained. Then you
untied the rope you'd wrapped around my waist
to keep me safe, watching as I wormed my way down
the dilapidated ladder. Springing from rung to rung,
you followed me with the grace of an acrobat.
I held the ladder steady, although it was unnecessary.

David Vancil

A Garden Outside Eden

The garden of my infirmities is crowded with flowers:
lily-of-the-valley from the marsh near Granddad's farm,
a trillium Grandma domesticated, the sweet alyssum
Mother planted along the path to our front door.
Violets and white clover in the grass announce
a casual approach to lawn maintenance.
The semicircular driveway is shaded by
white pine from a cottage on Lake Michigan.

I have not always been attentive to plants.
My first apartment was sporadically adorned
with green-grown gifts from those who did not know
that, thirsting after wisdom, I'd forget
to water them. The flowering cactus survived a full year.
At some point, one who visited stayed on.
The cut flowers of marriage died quickly;
we moved in mingled hope and fear to the next stage.

At a fix-up bungalow with rampant vegetation,
I unwound trumpet vine from maple tree limbs
and learned to kill aphids on roses with soapsuds.
I never knew when to prune hydrangea, but some blooms survived.
Circumstances too complicated to relate
delayed the new house more than twenty years.
Sometimes I expected to die from stress or exhaustion.
Fate laughed at such drama, sending arthritis and a pink slip.

In another apartment with an extra bedroom for the son,
a chance meeting sends up shoots that look like love.
On the far side of forty, I survive transplanting,
but the shockwaves keep us reeling together ten years.
When hope is gone, we find a vacant lot, converted farmland.
Digging deep for the foundation to build a home,
we unearth dormant seeds of thistle, morning glory, sassafras.
The next year we plant trees, then shrubs, finally flowers.

In late afternoon, I sit near a window. My neighbor
appears in green gloves to pull weeds and deadhead
her flowers. I recall when my body knelt with such grace.
My mind, no less eager for life, is confined by age
and attrition to the space of a garden. For all my desires—
for friendship, for marriage, for ambition—
the last transformation is watching them fade.

Ann Borger

Inside Earth

Leaving behind the sweltering heat of a
West Virginia July,
we crawl into the coolness of the cave.
On hands and knees, we humbly enter—
for this cave still belongs to Earth.
Its shell has not been broken open
for easy access with wide trails, guard rails,
guides and gaudy lights pointing out her pearls,
lit with unnatural orange and blue,
to anyone willing to pay five dollars for a ticket.

The ticket to this sanctuary is courage and sweat.
Climbing over slippery rocks like clumsy seals,
trudging through deep suctioning mud,
and squeezing through tight spots like bloated snakes,
with the reward of welcome exhaustion.
Stretched out flat in the soft caress of clay
facing darkness, at home in the earth's womb.
Silent but for blood rushing through ears and
the heartbeats of trusting companions.
At peace in the knowledge that together we are safe.
Forgetting the danger for a brief moment,
we gain union with Earth.

Until the chill sets in, forcing us to move,
countering hypothermia with a will to live.
Making it up the next ledge with a push from behind,
stretching for the hand reaching out from above,
suffering through an icy stream, we keep moving—
body heat surging once again.
Finally, relying on backup flashlights,
eyes feast upon familiar territory,
then sunlight intrudes into our darkness.
Bruised, aching, thirsty; muddy, yet exhilarated,
we emerge into the humid sweetness of the pasture,
wash in the creek, and warm ourselves in the bright sun.

Connie S. Tettenborn

Fireflies In My Hair

Nighttime
was a favorite time,
a place to go out
and just run upon soft night air,

quiet as a leaf
blending in the shadow,
free as I have never been.

No one to see me,
no one to tell me what to do.
Just me, my essence,
riding the breeze,
hitched to a star
with fireflies in my hair.

Some mourn the setting sun,
the gloaming, the end of day.

Not I.
I always liked the night,
the only time
free of cares.
No place to go.
No work to do.
My time to roam far and wide
within my mind.

No one to find me,
call me,
tell me.
Just me.
My heart.
My own.

Mary Ardeth Gaylord
October 4, 1954 ~ June 1, 2020

The Plant in My Office

is the first I've kept alive
more than a year
of the thirty I've breathed
there.

No flowers interrupt
long, green leaves,
lower ones drooping, the rest
reaching towards the absent
sky.

I'm unaware what kind
of plant resides with me,
nor whether it could grow
tree-sized if transported
to free soil or at least a bigger
pot.

Wanting water once
a week, shedding only a few
leaves at a time after they have
become tan ghosts of their former
selves, this plant's an easy roommate,
its sturdy brown base promising years
more.

I sometimes, though, mistake
its single drops of sticky sap
poised on any number of its stems
for tears, though there is no way
of knowing if my planted companion
cries more for its own sake or
mine.

                                   Joe Benevento

After I Left the Hospital Having Witnessed the Birth of My First Child

It was pouring rain at four in the morning on the fourth of June
and early March cold
that soaking summer of 1993; weeks later, the levee
would break and almost drown West Quincy,
but I was somewhere else,

flooded with the nearly thirty-eight years of my life
before this moment: the pre-teen years contemplating
the priesthood, mostly because I could not believe
any woman would ever want me, the eleven years
of my first marriage, where we might as well

have been celibate, so protective against pregnancy
my first wife. And the years swimming away
up to Aunt Flo's funeral in Tulsa, where I
witnessed the soothing dignity
of family, the mourning of my five cousins,

the honor they delivered in allowing me
to escort their feeble father through ceremonies
while they pall-bore their loved one to her final place.
In that sea of suits and ties and dark
dresses, I recognized my own children drowning,

but not too late for a life-
        saver, the lightning strike annulment no
betrayal, instead an inevitable stirring,
        a storm cycle designed before my beginning,
this rainy night bequeathing to me

my daughter's cries, already calling me by my nighest name.

                                        Joe Benevento

The Spiderweb

The room,
unused but not abandoned,
is anchored by tenuous threads
onto sill and wall and shelves
and leaning towers of books: a spiderweb.
Massive, tangled, chaotic, and yet
ominous in its simplicity,
it captures my attention.

Trancelike, I stare.
The web floats and billows
on an unseen draft and pulls me closer
with the desire to touch
its silken, breathing surface.

Suppressed thoughts a
white noise without focus
chart a jagged path in my brain.
I raise a hand in front of me,
attempting to brush away a spiritual fog
with fingers I no longer recognize.

Reading toward the web,
I hesitate, then stop
like an antique figure in bronze
recently unearthed,
frozen in a gesture.

What now?
Step forward or step back?
What dance is this, and who pulls the threads?
Am I the spider or the fly?
The dreamer or the dream?
Questions left unspoken
or at least unheard,
swallowed by silence.

Patrick Kalahar

Quality Control Work at the Copy-Cat Factory: Night Shift

Products made better elsewhere are stumbling along
the lurching line. I smash them with this hammer.
It's a job I came here for. After listless years of study
with a third runner-up—*years*, all chucked—I wanted
my place at the end of the line. Aptitude tests
& they gave me this spot. Since then, a raise—impossibly,
a lab coat, and a hammer-song to shape my time.

All implacable day, the tacky heave past: Kit Kat Clocks,
Beef Jerky Machines, Slap Chops, Pocket Fishermen,
Turbo Food Dehydrators. I smash them.
Breaks, I can take when I want. Absent my hammer,
all rolls into the pit the same, shattering
when they bottom. Day's end, I descend the blue-black
shadow, shovel errant smash, sweep the gradient.

Some days it's easy: heaps build up, sometimes topple
of their own despair and tumble to the river.
Some days there's time to watch them sink, adding strata
on yesterday's, last week's detritus. (I'm hoping
that I'm building a reef, rechanneling the course.
I hope one day to flood the factory floor.)

The buoyant keeps me wary; how *ought-nots* will drift
the rancid, blue-black current. I think they're fished out
downstream. Shards escaping, colorful,
asymmetrical, are selected by beaver,
round-tailed muskrats, otters, nutria, and
plastered into dams, dens, and burrows,
the inevitable, inexorable
next phase of rodent evolution.

Samuel Prestridge

Sin Eater

An upscale, failing strip mall, the August sun,
a burnished stopwatch. In his shades under
his beach umbrella, he's making his standing last
by being seen, not seeing. Spoken to, he aims
to ignore, meets questions with the slash of a thumb,
a speedy underscoring name, date, address
in thick, brushed scrawls:

GOING OUT OF BUSINESS!

I like that his job depends on not getting it done.
Avoid folks, he'll make rent. He can count on their ways
of not seeing panhandlers—if people think
the failure's his because he's bringing bad news,
that's probably alright. A Sin Eater's concern
was always the dead belly bedecked with small bowls
of boiled chicken, rankling beans, cold rice, cast-off bread.
Stricken generosities. Privacy to eat.

No one wants half-assed forgiveness, so he's allowed
to take his time, master gourmand of all-gone-wrong.

I could do that job.
                    Invisibility's bliss
the walked-past, glanced-at job of telling somebody
else's trouble. I envy his standing like a bollard
on the sidewalk. Also, I like that he's his own
boss, won't work weekends, and moves on to the next train wreck.
Living off failure means a steady payday.

And it could be worse. Across the street, wagging, hopping
as if he's befriending every goddamn car in the city,
a theater major, nine feet tall in his velveteen puppy suit,
shaking his purpled ass at traffic, his sign announcing

BIG PUPPY SALE!

Some breathless, heat-exhausted young pinhead
writhing to please, underpaid and overheated,
with nothing to look forward to but birth.

Samuel Prestridge

A Dog's Job of Work

(Brisa, *requiescat in pace*)

Having taken the front yard, the trees almost to their summits,
English ivy snakes, interweaves, tunnels beneath deadfall,
leaf rot, a rake left out last spring. It emerges as Gordian
tangles, strands too brittle for half tugs. Against such folderol,

Hank's élan has him grabbing rag ends from my hand,
tugging strands to ground,
wrangling, berserk, and digging straight down for roots.
I praise the dog,
his job of work, this deconstruction of knot, snarl, and tangle.
Above all not sorted, he hovers, hikes his leg, zings, negates

offending particulars on trash cans, tires, any smaller
dog—oracular, sure-fire, his eponymous persistence.
He attends. Where Maggie pisses, he sniffs and pisses the same
to show newcomers how thoroughly she's lied, how history

and process end at his decrial—methodologies, creeds,
professions, empiricists' smug bastions, metaphysics—all
met with his stream. Irrefutable, fluid as a hot God's
judgment, his nose for consequence, dissemblance, remedy, fraud.

Dog, keep me from intention, baffle, rote. From yearning, yearly
subscription to *Better Homes and Gardens*. Teach me the wrangle
and growl, the subjugating snarlings, tangles, unrakeable
and libertine, to asymmetrical cunning—the manglings

and tumblings requisite to howl against geometrical
containment. Rage at receptacles—cardboard boxes' hubris,
smug logos' filagree, all gnawed, soaked, worried down to wilting.
Demonstrate, I pray, the height, breadth, and depth of damn-fool daring
discernment, the knack for unaccepting unsniffed evidence
and all proofs unbitten and unbatted. Provide such ferule
as channels energies of nose, teeth, claw, and tear—your purview.
Share with me your verve. Deliver me from the Levitical.

Samuel Prestridge

41

Ideal Readers: A Poem for my Daughter

Sarah decides, casting about for a tattoo,
on lines in a poem I wrote for her: *I want
a pebble's worth of riot, footsteps on the moon.*

She gets it tattooed on her right foot, wears sandals
to her job bartending. It's summer. Co-workers
see the tat, want to see the poem. Sarah gives
them copies. Each picks a line, an image, goes
to the same tattoo parlor. Cooings and envy
abound as friends—and their friends' various buddies—
ask to see my manuscript, which they savage
into sentences, phrases, nouns, modifiers,
verbs, clauses adjectival *and* adverbial.

Expressions contort their ways through cognoscenti,
hangers on, denizens of the cultural blip.
Screeds, inked in swirly fonts. Freight their feet will carry
the rest of their lives. One by one, then rivulets
at a time, they troop downtown armed with a trenchant
image, a planned phrase, verses blooming on their feet.

Anonymous decades become a demitasse
of ink festooning ankles, soles, tops of feet, calves, toes,
slither from a tendon toward a heel.
Summer comes again. It's almost salmonesque,
the way they head uptown over the wheeling
weeks to the same boutique. The same tired shoe salesman
waits on them all. Hundreds he waits on, reading
their feet, taking in my manuscript,
no titles, no sequence—just ink and more women
coming, hundreds. He's reading. He's never read this much ...

*The lines, images coalesce the way a drop
of water takes in another, polarities
aligning, volume increasing surface tension.
Another drop assimilated. More tension.
No telling where the rupture will occur. No telling ...*

Weeks later, I'm out window shopping,
thinking leathers, prices, stitching, heels, and he steps
into sunlight, squinting, walks the block with me, quiet
at first. Then, fidgeting and almost hang-dogged, he says,
"I need to shake your hand. I'm damned if I know why."

Samuel Prestridge

Always, Her Bedside Lily

Does it simply await these faithful daybreaks
—each an event now as your years dwindle—
or is it the very force that awakens you,
the silent, stately perfection
that holds all the reason needed
to open again your eyes that so much
of the world has filled, eyes that so many
men's and women's eyes have prized

Alone, you greet this morning
serene and complete as the living art
that owes its life to your care

Strange, though, is it not
that its owing of this one life
casts you in its everlasting debt
for the years of lives it might have led
with its fellows dancing their saffron wave
in the wild bed below your window
where it bloomed its last
for the guileless mirror of your gaze,
and perhaps, if it stays its dying long enough,
the adorning and trumpeting of one more Easter
for you, ageless lover, risen in your loamy bed

Dan Carpenter

Sechura

Small islands of red-green
vegetation creep
across bare sands
& up the high
flanks of dunes

    the thin crust of
    snowy salt puddles
    imprinted by animals,
    this drying earth
    cracking deep, deeper

thicker thorn thickets
snag trash,
stubby grey grass
stipple the coarse
beige soil

roots, seeds long dormant
awakened for a short while

    dark patches where
    water had
    shimmered, where
    thin streams had
    flowed white

    & a stranded
    crimson lake ....

        When did it rain here
        to bring this desert
        back to life?

Lorraine Caputo

For Pat Fitzgerald
For Bobby

This renegade sleep
finds no part of me.
Another night gone.

Gabriel, blow your horn
to the muted drums
of distant angel wings.

We must trust
one shore to another
the maps we've made.

On a table for tomorrow's wake,
photographs I date in no special order.

I hold them in my hands
neither nervous nor cold, yet
shaking, nonetheless.

As if retouched by absence
now measured in spaces
that grow as wide as fate's arc.

Ever circling into dark days
with your light extinguished.

Sister Pat, sweet tears,
tears, tears I refuse to let
bitterness mock or taint.

It's raining outside.
Already I've enough
water to drown.

But it's not my time—
didn't think yours
would come before mine.

Sister Pat,
hear this whisper
anguish has given me.
My chain gang of words
failing to say
this rumor of goodbye.

My ink-dry pen
failing to note
blood remains in blood

even unto
the other
side.

Sister Pat,

walk the skies
in time,
I'll come.

We must trust
one soul to another
maps we've made

We must follow
one soul to another
these maps we've made.

Rp Verlaine

My Girl

These are my hopes for you, my girl.
First that you will grow like a country rose—
a perfect mix of wildness and beauty
with a flare of red fire just like your mother.
Delicate and lovely but armored with thorns.

May you be like the willows,
tall, mighty, and graceful, giving beauty to the world.
And, most of all, not afraid to dance in the storm.

Be like the little poppy, small but sassy,
and you will stand out, never getting lost in a field of clover.

Like the bellflowers, you will be light and airy,
unshackled to convention and shouting with imagination.

Above all, be yourself and grow into the one you want to be,
my wildflower. Be brave and run with the wind,
watching the dragonflies sail across the sky.
Your inner light is true beauty, and your heart courageous,
dreaming dreams that belong to you and you alone.
Take time to stroll the meadows,
and let nature and you become one.
These are among the countless hopes I have for you, my girl.

W. B. Cornwell

The Worth of a Family Tree

Some may ask what a family tree is—what is the point.
Is it beautifully illustrated images with names and dates
of those otherwise forgotten?
Is the purpose of this chart just to save our ancestors
from being ravaged by the dust of time?
Is a family tree that cobweb-garnished hallway in Grandma's house
with peeling wallpaper and lined with silver and brass frames
encasing faces frozen in time like fossils in amber?
Or are family trees compiled from shoeboxes from the attic,
the ones full of old letters, marriage documents,
and Great-Grandpa's journal
he thought no other human eyes would see?

All those options are viable and beautiful,
but really, a family tree is a living thing,
full of those connected by countless generations
of love stories, tales of fearless pioneers
and shared heartbreak.

Over time, branches spread to the four corners of the earth,
yet they are all rooted in a tapestry far greater than we will ever know.
Our duty is to water the tree,
to help stories and names be remembered,
to pay homage to those who came before us,
or we will face the same fate—
to be forgotten and swallowed by another generation who didn't care.
I, for one, will water the tree.
I will remember. I will be a proud carrier of their legacy.
Even if I stand alone in this task,
I will stand on the shoulders of those who came before.

W. B. Cornwell

Grandpa's Garden

Hidden by leaves
hugging the ground
far beneath even my low, preschooler's knees,
bold red fruit—
unknown, unseen, untasted—
beckoned without a word

till my grandfather
brought us over to stoop
and sweep aside the beaded leaves
with the backs of our hands
to sight and seize, this time,

strawberries.

Like the tomatoes
(and cherry tomatoes
which my brothers had already yielded to me,
since I, with my freckles and beacon of hair,
was also the smallest red globule around),
they moistened our throats
and slobbered our chins
suddenly, lusciously, scrumptiously,
with a heavenly sweetness
unlike earthy tomatoes',
for they were,
after all,
strawberries
best picked and savored
after a rainy spell,
Grandpa, with his accent, taught us.

After wiping our chins and cheeks
of strawberry and tomato,
Grandpa gave us a tour
of the rest of the plot of his vast back yard,

much of which rose in well-kempt rows
like characters in a printer's typesetting block,
but some of which sprawled like scraggly free-form verse
as diverse
as the Old and New Worlds:

tough kale, sharp chicory, inscrutable okra,
curt semi-sour grapes,
communal sprouts Brussels
(each ball or bulb stacked neatly on a neighbor),
and garlic, potent as a white-haired sorcerer;
beyond them, tart raspberries (prickly yet delightful)—

all now parts of me.

My brother and I still savor
that summer the rain
decided to stop
and our grandfather
picked up from the kitchen table
a hexagonal, glass saltshaker
small enough to match a preschooler's palm,
and hooked his index finger as if to say
in the international language of love and silence

Follow me

and we followed him

and the moment he placed
in each of our palms
our own, individual,
earth-shattering

tomato.

James B. Nicola

Rudbeckia Girl

Before you worked in the city, you grew up on a farm.
People react with surprise when they find that out,
but it takes smarts to grow food.
For a while,
you left the job you have now
to weed and water herbs,
vegetables,
and flowers
to sell at a roadside stand.
That was after you grew a baby.
It was sweaty, back-aching work,
but you got to be the first to see the Lisianthus bloom,
so pretty and round
just like you, growing that second baby.
But you're more of a Rudbeckia girl.

You communed with geese at dusk
when they came 'round in the fall
to scavenge the last kernels of corn in the next field over.
It was a red and blue time, mixed with
pink
and yellow
and orange.
Now you work in information again.
People are surprised when they find out you worked on a farm.

                         Brenda Ross

Why the Prophets were Right

Copula for an eye,
remoteness promotes meditation.
We would like to offer you this.
The river mouths are rarely
just the imitation of sound.
Can't see to feel here.
Like a river, you can choose
the indirect route,
almost winding back on yourself.
Erosion, the brain disease,
is avoided by statuesque ladders.
See them climb into an ambivalent sky.
Always what ladder you choose depends
on the availability of its satellite.

Colin James

Detasseling

The field doesn't need a mouth
to swallow you. The wall of mature corn stalks
closes as you enter & it's like you were never

here. Your skin is licked raw by thousands of dry husks.
Blotchy rash of microscopic cuts & relentless sunburn
itches all summer. Ghost of a breeze whispers

in the swaying tassels overhead. Thrust your hand
above the crops. Your outstretched fingers
look like someone drowning. Thick mud sucks

your boot with each step. Remember
your grandparents' advice; lift your heel
with force to snap the wet soil's grasp.

On your way home, identical cornfields
flank every road. Drive for miles
but feel like you have gone

nowhere. Exhausted, untie your crusted
black laces. Add yours to the row of
muddy boots on the front porch.

Joseph Kerschbaum

Root Cultivate Bloom

Leaving the door unlocked behind her,
singing wistfully to herself,
she inspects the whirling insects
on her new tomato plants.

Their presence unsettles her heart
and unhinges her fettered mind.
The bugs remind her of her husband
ruining beauty, marring the future.
Something delicious will grow, regardless.

Her daughter calls from the house:
the soup is boiling over!
She rushes in and salvages dinner.
There is some comfort to be had.

There is some comfort to be had
in love whose promise isn't wholly dashed.
There is some comfort to be had in family
and familiar rituals. Repair survives remorse.
The garden will, like dreaming, soldier on.

Bill Yarrow

Dohilla

Tetrapod Trackway on Valentia Island, Co. Kerry, Ireland

As the sun begins to drop into the Atlantic
on the north edge of Valentia Island,

we turn away from the view of a lifeboat
swinging at anchor in front of Beginish.

Following dead-end dirt roads,
we've spent a luckless afternoon

searching for Dohilla, then
we spot a makeshift wall

of upright flagstones,
following a gravel path to its end.

Below us are spaced indentations
in a shelf at the edge of the sea, and

though the incoming tide splashes us, on hands
and knees, we crawl down for a better look.

Long shadows bring into sharp relief
footprints set in the concrete of time.

I trace with my forefinger the grooves
where the creature—a miniature crocodile—

dragged its heavy tail in mud
before it hardened into stone.

I fit the ball of my fist into one of the prints,
and just as darkness closes in on this islet,

I struggle ashore for the first time,
blinking away saltwater tears,

stars flashing in celebration,
my arrival, our beginnings here.

Carlos Reyes

Some San Francisco Trees

1.
Leaves like yellow-orange cling peach slices
fill out and make fulsome the tree;
raking is not what most of them are for.
They are still in their brightest element,
but a homeowner has arranged a scarf of early-fallen ones
around its roots as though to keep them warm.

2.
Like Sally Rand's large ostrich-plume fans,
the tips of branches of three close trees
sway, dip, waver, flare, and reassert themselves
against strong ocean wind from five miles west.

I see no obvious meaning in these trees
whose trunks, like legs of a tall elephant,
stand in square sidewalk openings of earth.

Disturbed portions falling back against others
sigh until wind ceases and each bough is silent.

3.
There is a tree on Eureka
between Twenty and Twenty-first,
an ordinary tree, special to me
because its canopy two stories high
umbrellas so massive-delicately
that when you walk beneath,
your eyes are lifted up
to see its simple leaves disclose the sky.

Eureka is the street I choose
often as I can to undergo that tree.
And yet I have not stayed to stand
half long enough, but stroll
two houses down to view a daisy plant,
its arrested burst of bloom that cannot last.
But still, the visited tree
companions me.

Jonathan Bracker

Clasp and Loop

She has a gold necklace
with a clasp and a loop
the clasp goes around the loop
and embraces it
I must help her
put it on
from behind
my fingers are clumsy
they struggle with
its delicacy
its imbalance
whatever it is
that makes her think
I can do it better
but I get it wrong
her fingers appraise
its correctness
its fluidity around her neck
the gold chain is twisted
she says
it is wrong
I do it over
it is still wrong
from behind her
I know she smiles
she places the loop where
the clasp was
and has me do it over
I repeat the procedure
not knowing how this will make
any difference
her fingers run up and down the chain
to ascertain the necklace's uniformity
she spins around
with that smile
my fingers
thickset and fumbling
reach down and grasp her hand
tight as a clevis

Paul Smith

Pastoral

Mother would take us on bird walks
it was just us two
until other neighborhood kids
tagged along in the nearly vacant blocks
of our suburb
she pointed out thrushes, tanagers, blue jays
and robins
lots of robins
she even kept a diary of when
the first robin showed up each spring
a date that got earlier
each year
she told us to keep still
but had a way of drawing people to her
lowering her head
speaking softly
she wasn't big on eye contact
but she leaned your way
to make sure you knew
she listened
she could identify the robins
carrying twigs in their beaks
to build nests
one year we just stopped
I played Little League
the others wandered away
mother still kept her diary
noting the first robin's arrival
till she stopped that too
maybe it was that the robins
stopped
stopped going south
I no longer played ball
the kids moved away
mother died
trees got cleared and
houses got built on the empty lots
somewhere a wren builds a nest
you can see it if you listen

Paul Smith

Advice from Mary Oliver

"Be astonished," she says
in almost every poem.
As if
this is something so basic
and essential that it can be contained
In just two words.
As if
without preparation or rehearsal
anyone can exercise this capacity
for alertness and complete abandonment
to the small, the ordinary,
and otherwise unremarkable.
As if
the only thing healing needs
to take root in the wounded
and spread across the whole long
day ahead is round-eyed wonder.
It is, perhaps, the hardest discipline
to practice—harder than eating right
or exercising a little every day
or spending money wisely
or handing over forgiveness,
that lovely shell from the salty, bottomless
ocean, or worse, admitting you are wrong.
All these things would be easier,
would be easier, of course,
if astonishment dosed our moments,
like a cup of cold water thrown into the shower
while we are wet and naked and unable to defend
ourselves from the bright and sudden shock.

We would be less likely to stumble, I think,
having been brought awake this way.
And because we would see the snakes in the grass,
they wouldn't frighten us—frighten *me*—
so much, the silky length of their muscled bodies
long, lovely words writing themselves under an invisible pen:
Awe, tomorrow, right now.

Deborah Zarka Miller

Before the Wind

Like this, he said, and we watched him pulling the tiller
toward him, heading off the wind, filling the spinnaker.
It was a soft wind, and the sun was endless.
I wondered if he, too, had struggled to

> build a self

or if he'd been embraced by a family who would embrace me.
You move the tiller in the opposite direction
from the pitch of the waves.
People think you can relax when you are before the wind. No,

> you have to balance.

Behind him, a colony of gulls swirled, darting in and out of the bay,
seizing small fish, seeming to suggest
we should pepper him with questions.
But the sun, the sea, and the rocking boat

> left us sluggish and mute.

I daydreamed I was lying on the deck
and the gunnels grew up and softly stretched over to enfold me.
The tiller swayed without me. The spinnaker billowed without wind,
blue and red and white. No thoughts permeated my brain.

> Then I woke

and saw the moment: I could reach out, maybe touch his hand,
initiate a process that could maybe lead to love;
or I could bask in the numbing sun and dream. I sat balancing the two.
Does everyone understand? he asked. Brushing his leg,

> I said yes.

Elizabeth Hill

My Last Afternoon with Gramma Hill

1968: My Grandparents' Summer House

The manicured lawn stretched down to
the beach, the dock, and the harbor.
A giant swing hung from the rafters of the wrap-around porch.
When we arrived at Gramma's house, we went straight to the kitchen
where Jessie and Eulalia, her live-in help,
fawned over us, as usual,
giving us home-made brownies and Coca Cola,
which we otherwise weren't allowed to have.

Grampa's study was a womb.
Curtains semi-drawn.
Dark with red oriental rugs.
Grampa's huge retirement locomotive clock
told time as the side rods swept back and forth.
Grampa sat on the sienna sofa. We snuggled up and
he let us push his hernia around
like a game of whack-a-mole; you push it down one place,
it pops up another.
Grampa was in the cavalry in World War One.
His picture hung on the wall:
handsome and jaunty in uniform and jodhpurs,
with his riding crop tucked under his arm.
My Gramma's parents thought she married beneath her station.

When I was almost too young to understand,
my mother told me my older brother was a genius.
I asked, "What am I?" She said,
"You're good at stick-to-itiveness."

Gramma took out her special toys for me,
as she always did.
My brother wasn't interested. My sister was too small.
We played alone in the living room,
the sun streaming through the French windows,
the salmon and robin's-egg blue oriental carpet stretching out forever.

The antique clavichord stood at our end of the room, with
it's delicate inlaid wood.
Nobody played it.

Gramma sat in a light-orange dress with her dark-brown chignon,
coughing intermittently,
her huge brown eyes dwelling on me
through the wisps of cigarette smoke.
When she watched me play,
I was second to no one.
I grew in size. I was boundless.
I was wide-eyed and off-balance.
Gramma's toys transported me.
They dated from the turn of the century when she was a child.
Gramma's dollhouse was my favorite. Everything was handmade,
and all the beautiful things worked.
Scissors no longer than a fingernail opened and closed.

The dollhouse was exquisite.
There was an Edwardian porcelain lady doll,
three inches tall, perfectly proportioned,
chest thrust out like a robin,
dark-green silk dress, plaid sash,
grand straw hat, jaunty at an angle, with a tiny cerulean blue plume
and a working parasol.
Pewter cutlery no longer than the tip of my little finger.
A white wooden bathroom sink with an ivory plaque on the back
no bigger than my thumbnail, etched in black script:

An intricate cut glass punch bowl, one inch in diameter.
An ivory filigreed sewing table with an opening top.
Two porcelain maids in plain dark blue dresses.
Tiny knitting needles with a tiny woolen project.
A working manual sewing machine, one- and one-half inches high.

At seventy-eight, Gramma was dying of emphysema.
She was the first person I knew who had died.
I was eight and was not taken to the hospital or the funeral.
I did not know what an excruciating death it had been,
but I understood that I would never see her again.
I would never feel her all-encompassing gaze again.
I was no longer boundless, but I had the toys.

I inherited Gramma's extraordinary toys and kept them safe
in my childhood room. I assembled the dollhouse and left it on display.

In 1995, my cousin's prepubescent children stayed
at my childhood home,
refugees from a vicious divorce.
They saw my perfect dollhouse
and systematically destroyed it.
They denuded my Edwardian lady. They pulled
the legs off tables. They tore the knitting needles apart.
They chipped off all the paint and enamel from the walls,
furniture, bowls, plates, and pitchers.

Even now, old enough to be a grandmother myself,
viewing the remnants of the dollhouse causes me physical pain.
The marauders were Gramma's own great-grandchildren,
but they never played under her kind brown eyes
and never tasted Jessie and Eulalia's brownies and Coke.

Elizabeth Hill

My Passionate Affair

At first,
I didn't kiss the daffodils.
I slowly touched each petal
with my fingers,
picked bunches of Lillies of the Valley,
held their blossoms
close to my face.
I breathed in,
holding the deep aroma
of their fragrance
until my lungs gasped for air.
Wild violets beckoned me
to come closer, lie down with them
in the soft, warm, green grass.
Ferns wildly danced in the breeze,
tickling my ankles,
giving me goosebumps.
Purple irises opened their wombs,
and tall red poppies reached out,
took my hands.
A trellis of clematis whispered,
"Tie my loose strands.
Don't let them fall."
Every new bloom begged
to be caressed, and I,
like a long-lost lover,
awakened
from a deep, cold sleep,
am now alive, making love
with spring.

RM Yager

I Can't Dance

I can't dance
or hold a tune.
My jokes fall flat
and jump shot sucks.

Never could hit the curve.
My vote doesn't seem to count
and too many days it seems my prayers
fall silent, as soundless as dust settles onto the floor.

Still, I try to hold my part of the world together
with a few words and a measure of grammar,
what we have known since Coleridge as
best words, best order, along with a

chance metaphor that falls to earth,
takes root and begins to sprout.

James Green

Elegy for a Bachelor Farmer

Neighbors marveled at his harvests.
Year after year, best yield at the Ardwell Co-op.

No machinery on the place he couldn't fix.
Rarely did he buy a new part.

Most came from what he called the parts department,
a collection of retired implements behind the barn.

And some, the ones that needed sorting and sizing,
he shelved inside the shed—nuts and bolts, bearings and such.

Stern as the deacons at church, spare with words,
he kept only such company as necessary,

and none for the heart, preferring (he once said) silence
of his own making to the kind that follows a quarrel.

One day, plowing the east forty, the tractor purring
like a kitten, what was left of his heart sputtered, coughed,

and stopped.

Slumped over the steering wheel, he mustered the strength,
and presence of mind, to disengage the hand clutch,

its lever slipping effortlessly forward so that the man
and his machinery stalled dead in their tracks.

No one knows when it happened.
When they found him, he was still at the wheel,

stiff as a plough blade, the gas tank empty,
furrows so straight you'd sworn he used chalk lines,

the field only half turned.

                                        James Green

97. Coming to Terms & Goodbye

An atheist faces his own death

Wait until I have to say goodbye.
Don't rush; I'm a philosophical professor
facing my own death on my own time.
It takes longer to rise to kick the blankets back.
I take my pills with water and slowly lift
myself out of bed to the edge of my walker.
Living to age ninety-seven is an experience I share
with my caretaker and so hard to accept.
It's hard for youngsters who have not experienced
old age to know the psychology of pain.
You can't put your socks on or pull
your own pants up without help anymore—
thank God for suspenders.
"At a certain point, there's no reason
to be concerned about death. When you die,
no problem. There's nothing."
But why in my loneness—teeth stuck
in with denture glue, my daily pillbox complete,
and my wife, Leslie Josephine, gone for years—
does it haunt me?
I can't orchestrate, play Ph.D. anymore,
my song lyrics running out, my personality
framed in a gentler state of mind.
I still think it necessary to figure out
the patterns of death; I just don't know why.
"There must be something missing
from this argument; I wish I knew.
Don't push me. Please wait; soon
is enough to say goodbye.
My theater life now shared, my last play
coming to this final curtain, I give you
grace, "the king of swing," the voice of
Benny Goodman is silent now,
an act of humanity passes, no applause.

Michael Lee Johnson
Dedicated to the memory of Herbert Fingarette,
November 2, 2018 (aged 97).

71

An Accident

I had an accidental garden once.
Thrown-out leftover fruits and vegetables
were food for the chickens,
or so I thought,
but a few of those seeds
snuck their way into the ground,
and one day as I walked by that patch of dirt,
sprouts were peeking up at me,
an unexpected pleasure
that left me not knowing how to feel.
But as quickly as I noticed them,
watered them a few times,
they were gone,
wilted by the hot sun and
chickens pecking at them.
So I made a vow to be more careful of what I threw out in the yard,
not wanting another accidental garden
just to have it taken away.
Instead, becoming intentional,
I found a plot for my future vegetation
far enough away from birds,
with perfect lighting that won't scorch the plants
but help them grow strong.
Tilling the land,
fertilizing it,
I often find myself sitting in the middle
of my little patch of heaven,
sifting soft soil through my fingers,
contemplating blooms
that will soon speckle this haven.
These thoughts fill me with joy
and numb my melancholy
over my lost accidental garden.

Kaela Hinton

The Hidden Spring

We were just starting out.

A frozen November
wedding outside.

You wore a rabbit fur coat.

Christmas lights burned
all around the castle.

Everyone we wanted to see
was there.

Your lipstick matched
the red rose and paper flower
bouquet in your hands.

A bag-piper played
She Moves Through the Fair.

There were words spoken,
but they've been forgotten.

I'd been hiking all day.

They told me to look for the spring
in the holler by the shooting range.

I saw nothing in the cold there.

The timothy grass,
dried and shorn, snapped
like straw underfoot.

I almost twisted my ankle in a rut
that could have once held water.

I followed the rut
to an outcrop of limestone
next to a scrub dogwood bush.

Fiddlehead ferns and lichens
sprouted among the stones.

A pale spring beneath a crust of ice
bubbled from a hillside hollow.

You took my arm.

I punched through the ice
with three fingers.

Your hands were so warm,
a fire in my own.

A shiver ran to my elbows
as I cupped the water to my lips.

There were rings exchanged,
we kissed and began.

I have never tasted anything
so cold, so pure.

Timothy Geiger

The Plant-Killer

He came to mow the grass and trim the hedge
but cut the jasmine too close to the ground
then forced azalea blooms into a box that
hugged the house and matched a row of holly
by the fence. He swept the fallen leaves into
small heaps beneath the trees I had planted
long ago, but this smothered them to death,
and so, I had to let him go. He charged me
thirty silver pieces.

Mary Harwell Sayler

How Many Roads

A trip around the world before
I die would have to include all
the roads I've ever walked in this lifetime.

I want to see one more time that three-
dip highway on the way to Grandma's,
and the gravel road that
goes down the hill where she could
watch for our car.

The gravel road crossing the creek
where I played in summer,
where we fetched water from the spring.

And once again, please, the low-water
bridge across Mill Creek where we
used to wash our Model-A Ford
on a hot summer day. Where I could sit
with bare feet in cool water.

The highway to Bird Tavern outside
Anchorage where I spent many
delicious hours with my married lover.

The road leading out of Elmendorf
Air Force Base, my eyes drawn to
Chugach Mountain Range like magnets
to steel. Where I learned to express
gratitude for my eyesight.

So many roads taken. I am not
a weary traveler—I am blessed
with a heavy dose of wanderlust.

Please, just one more visit to Times Square
or a walk along the canals of Venice.
More time in Paris. More time.
My eyes are greedy for more.

Sandra de Helen

Through a Window, April

Each day the view
into the woods is more
obscured as leaves unfold,
gather their wits about them, and
open fully to receive light.

Each day the fence
becomes more of a barrier
as vines wrap and weave
themselves around metal
wires until the forsythia drips
over the top piping, explodes
in droplets of yellow until
the fence itself is a living thing,
now lush emerald green and gold
in its transformation.

Each day more birds
linger on the swing set,
assess the woods, flit to its trees,
seeming to search out
the best spot, the finest perch,
the most promising home in this
newly verdant place. They, like us,
turn toward sunlight, bask in it.
We preen and smooth our wings
together, ready for flight.

Mary Sexson

The Unlikely Gardener

Two days spent doing what I never do, what has never come
naturally to me, what I am not good at, hands in dirt, flats
of flowers all around me, random pots scattered about.

Too unskilled to dig directly into the ground, I meet the earth
halfway, filling clay pots with loamy dirt from bags seasoned
with miracle pellets, destined to grow giant flowers at will.

I have chosen ones they say you cannot kill, that
no matter what happens between buying the flats and my planting
of them in the receptacles, they will live and flourish, spread and fill

all the spaces I have left open. I try to remember
the overheard secrets from my green-thumb friends who talk
of moving hostas from one part of a yard to another as if it were

as easy as moving your feet. They plant bushes that thrive
for years, tend gardens that could feed a neighborhood, and cut
roses to make bouquets for vases on their own tables.

Their world, my labyrinth, this place I cannot navigate,
and yet here I am, sweaty and bent, my fingernails respectfully dirty.

Mary Sexson

Jiggle the Landscape

Yes, yes,
there is such a thing
as a dinnerplate dahlia
served up in every Latin color imaginable,
but this is a begonia,
and by size alone
should be allowed
to join the table.

Suspended from a swinging basket,
the cartoon-colored
bosomy blossoms
jiggle the landscape green,
paired up the same way
I used to make colors in school,
scribbling one crayon atop the other,
blending into something
I didn't know before.

Roger Camp

Enchanted Garden

At twilight, puffs of blue and marigold
sprout between brilliant grass spears of forest and celery green.
Boulders form natural mud basins for wildflowers.
Tucked between rocks, old crock pots fill with rainwater.
Wandering duck mates, Sophia and Harry, stop to drink a spell.

A tree trunk surrounded with toadstools invites:
come and linger for a while,
share a cup of tea, a carafe of wine,
recollections, laughter, intimate conversations
that trail through the wee hours drifting into silence.
The surrounding wildlife lulled by human voices
strain to eavesdrop for the next spoken word.

Cast stone angels play hide and seek
in the shadows among the rose bushes,
and everything … everything that my daughter plants
blooms and gloriously glistens in her garden.

Deep in the night,
deer spring across the meadows,
peek in bedroom windows.
A giant turtle emerges from a murky green pond,
slowly ambles across the way,
slips silkily into a secluded pond,
the moonlight traces its path.

Early morn, blue herons fly overhead,
a great span of wings across the sky.
Eyes search for a wayward rabbit
as squawking ducks dive into the pond,
hover under a cleft rock.
A stray tuxedo cat casts slit sun-beamed eyes
towards the sudden movement of leaves,
his ear cocked at the sound of feet
swishing on the cobblestones.

Judith A. Lawrence

The Passionate Gardener

Early one morning,
I carried my teacup to the deck
overlooking my small
unattended rocky garden.
I saw earth upturned
in a curious strategic design,
weaving around old rose bushes
and disenchanted peonies,
my daughter's hands deep in dirt,
her shoes caked in mud,
transplanting flowers one by one,
a determined look on her sunbaked face.

For a week I held my tongue,
doubting restoration
while marveling at her resoluteness,
watching from my kitchen window
as she tended reluctant strays,
a clucking, scolding mother
to misbehaving children,
fussing over the few
who dared to challenge her will.

Over time, the garden began to bloom.
As if by royal command,
brilliant purples, pale yellows,
delicate pinks, and passionate reds
shyly revealed themselves,
standing taller with each new sunrise,
giving rise to the belief
the following spring would produce
a tumbling patchwork flower garden
out of rocky terrain,
offering fresh cuttings
for new beginnings.

Judith A. Lawrence

Matri Vox

Her thumb
Crossing my brow against the dreams to come.

~~James Merrill

She stands just beyond the edge of my dream
As if to whisper you are not yet the reader of this poem,
As if to whisper—without sound so much
As with the faint aroma of rose on her breath,
Apricot rose, tea rose, English, bloom
I have tended two summers
The catalogue called Jude the Obscure
And so thick were it red
You might think it meat—
As if to whisper you are not yet the reader of this poem.

And though I must put my hands to my face,
My fingers having earlier in the evening
Plucked the fallen, the fragrant clumps of petals—
Like pairs of puppies' ears to the touch—
Stained the skin with their scent,
Though my lids are closed,
For a time beneath them
My eyes are open
And I know you are not yet the reader of this poem.

You are not yet the reader of this poem.
This is the pristine poem, the lines without words
To say them, the words without letters
To form them, the letters without ink, ink without substance.
It is the ink of dreamless sleep.
What it does not say is what it means,
Meaning silence is the mother
As much as is the muse
Just as the rose is to its lingering scent,
Which shall cease,
Meaning she shall be heard
Though not seen, not felt,
Before the poem has begun.

Karl Elder

Innocence

On through the darkening of the seeds
and the bronze equinox
I remember the brightness of days ~W.S. Merwin

before the winters
    the sweet scent of apples
baking in Gram's kitchen
and the *pie crusts are fragile* lesson
    and the one about
the rusty screen door
and the swinging davenport creak
and cicada screeches from up the apple tree
    where mystery comes from
and between its limbs the Nancy Drew lesson
    how fiction rescues

before the Newark riots
    a summer thunder five miles
from Mom and Dad's
    before Phil Benn next door
killed in Vietnam and Billy McGuire
from homeroom and before
    the Northeastern black-out
and our fall-out shelter roofless
    and before Mom's suicide note
another roofless threat
    and a scary German nanny

after the summers
    cornhusking and angel-hair
whispers of things unseen
    a hummingbird in my palm
and the smooth tree bark with the sun's heat
    sleep with no bad dreams

Kathy O'Fallon

Three Is Not a Crowd

Steel shovel's a T-junction planted in clay.
Robin squats on the handle-roost,
red breast a cherry pie ripe to bursting with Solfeggio song. He mapped
    as close as spit as you spoke in tongues & silence

The year of your missing,
    Alexandrina's eyes & ears flew half-mast

She'd see a flutter of wings as her gardening gloves planted aubergines,
    sunflowers, Jacobite roses, but it would be a wren, chaffinch, blue tit.
She wondered did you have enough grubs, bugs, seeds
    from baked apple earth? Were your claws a sunward statue?

The year of your returning,
    you stood an arm away, regular as prunes

Head an angle-poise lamp, you tweeted,
"I've been busy mud-cup nesting
    with my egg-nester." Robin twittered to Robina, "It's safe.
This Goddess of Nature, she told me stories, unearthed worms, fed me
    sunflower seeds, peanuts,
    pumpkin seeds with wells of water to slurp & preen in."
Robina's blackcurrant eyes wary,
    she winged down from a branch of magnolia
    blossom to wrestle with Alexandrina's emerald shoelace

Mandy Beattie

Church Street

The street I live on now
is the same street where I grew
into the sensitive creative
I am now. In a quiet small town
where stray cats and squirrels
are more frequent travelers than cars,
this street paved my way to escape
an unexciting place. Looking for
adventures when I was eighteen,

I never dreamed I would be summoned back at sixty,
making this street my home
one more time, moving my life
from Washington Street in Indy
where a squirrel or cat never dare cross,
let alone walk the middle of that road.
A street where the whirring of traffic
and emergency sirens became background
noise to my busy city life. Not now.

On Church Street, I can count on one hand cars
passing by daily, the sound of sirens
replaced by freight trains rumbling
a mile away. Geese head to the Mississinewa
(river, not the tavern) just three blocks south.
The street is vacant of huge Elm trees that lined my childhood
as I rode my bike back and forth to Grandma's
house one block west. Now, her familiar
house is for sale again.

Through the picture window, chirp, chirp, chirp
breaks the silence. The Northern Cardinal pair
arrive again—I've come to recognize them.
More birdsong overhead as sparrows and chickadees
aim for the feeders.
I worry for stray cats I feed on my front porch, too.
Sissy and Tilly are pregnant again, and I wonder
how many more mouths I can fill.

Lylanne Musselman

Stoical Gardening

The passionflower is not at all philosophical.

It flings a spirograph of purple threads, opens
its lemony wheel of pollen pouches to a naturalist
who doesn't have the wing-beat of a three thousandth
of an ounce fuzzed body, for one buzzy shuffle dance
on pistils and stamens.

A stoical gardener controls what she can and ignores
the rest, like the rain forest-mined sapphires
in the lobes of her ears.

When she saw it going, thoughts of possible loss
excited delight awhile in the long-gone bee.
And now there's a duty to be useful.

She takes a brush and scissors from flower to flower.
Tickles anther tips where grains of pollen stick.
Or cuts a bundle for pushing, unnaturally but poetic.

Outside a poem, nothing leafy needs to fill the deeps
of human longing. The vine will be itself.
Without our hunger, its perfumed fruit incidental.
Still, a poem needs our need for leafless namings
to remediate, where possible, the ache of vacancies.

Carrie Weinberger

Toward

Where am I walking? Now the red maple flares in the sun.
Then blue damselfly perches on a reed.
Briny August wind skitters off the ocean.

Each *ksana*—blink of time smaller than a second—
holds the speck of destination. No backtracking.
How can one keep up with this? Can't, and yet.

Hit the road, Jack, and don't you come back no more, no more,
no more, no more. But don't forget the time itch,
the ball of gnats in the singsong sun.

Now a swollen grape bursts on the vine, then a jacaranda bloom
falls, the dog snaps at a bottle-green fly and misses.
Here. There. Everywhere. Nowhere. No more.

Time unzips, water-lily style. Now the flick of a fish fin. Then
cessation of cicadas. I scratch my arm. That's it. A million *ksanas* gone.
Can you hear the creaky old screen door slam?

Regina O'Melveny

A *ksana* is a Sanskrit word in the Buddhist sutras for approximately one seventy-fifth of a second;
essentially, an imperceptibly small amount of time.

Pinky Notes

A poem dedicated to the cherry tree, the banana key, and to growth as a musician

The next time, I would ask that you please consult
before writing a C-Db slur for an oboe;
the normal keys don't lend themselves to your notation.

Even Hindemith knew that.

As Monty Don would know better than to cover the grass
with a four-inch-thick layer of pine straw
until it dies from beauty's sardonic asphyxiation.

Yet I also consider this,

On a walk in a new breeze among blossoming cherry petals,
the sound of skateboards pummeling their trunks,
they began their vertical lives before you arrived, day by day,

Turning them into curved remnants of their former selves, slow crescents,
days turn to weeks, flowers borne of a banana-key bloomer,
stronger, hardier, and my only salvation on page three of your piece.

Robert Simon

Rootman

Rootman lifted the bale as if it were air,
pointed to the other one: Can you get that?
I was in my late forties; he three decades older.
(I had to divide my bale into thirds.)
We fed his tilapia in the murky pond:
They like it this way. See. There they are,
and small mouths poked out their heads.
In his plot of sugar cane, he cut off two pieces,
started chewing on his, and handed me mine.
Never been to a dentist. Never had a toothache.
Sugar cane does the trick. He had prefect teeth.
I was already minus two with three cavities.
Come on, he said. Let's get something to eat.
We entered his house and then his cave,
and he reached up to pull at a few of the roots:
He cut pieces of malanga, taro, and yuca,
swollen and ready for his pot of boiling water.
Here's one you can chew right now, but don't swallow.
While we waited, he said, Let me teach you mancala,
and we played the game with seed pods
on a board carved from thick roots,
until morning went to afternoon, and I never beat him.

Michael H. Brownstein

Word or Bloom

Not until you watered
your husband's English

garden did you consider
it much. Not until you

turned on the faucet,
held the hose nozzle in

your own hand, stood
in the dying heat

of the day out of love
for him, gone on holiday

without you, did you
see the plants not just

as landscape, but as
children of summer.

Not until you felt the cool
spray you offered them

against your own body
did you know what it is

to nurture a plant, to care
for it as you would care

for a child, disabled and
mute, knowing through

some miracle or mystic
means, that love will be

returned to you with or
without word or bloom.

Mary M. Brown

All of Us Growers

Some sow a field of wheat and pray they make
a profit, buy another tractor to plow the earth
again, feeding children they will never know.
Others start a scatter garden, tossing seeds
like confetti onto unmade beds, trusting God's
grace will compensate for work they've left

undone. A grower learns that pruning leaves
from plants will help them thrive, will make
them blossom and survive the most ungodly
storm. And there are those who bypass earth
altogether, tend air plants, stick melon seeds
onto paper towels, in eggshells, waste no

time digging through some dark unknown
to wait for sprouts. Some planters believe
if they focus only on the strongest seedlings
they will reap the greatest reward. They make
the old mistake of forgetting the unearthly
will of green things to lean toward goodness,

light and life. Ancient Greeks called on gods—
Demeter, Attis, Cronus, Hermes—known
for their powers to coax herbs from earth,
and their entreaties worked; green leaves
returned in spring like an urge, life remade
each season, regrown, like those other seeds

that in a surge of passion, love, were sewn
in fertile wombs. We raise children godly
as steeples, temples, broken, unbroken, made
to grow skyward, to point us toward knowledge
and beauty, the only inheritance we leave
them when we die is the whole of our earthly

treasure. We not only grow food but unearth
spirits, tend selves the size of mustard seeds,
nurture them until they are ready to leave
the cribs we have made them and go to God-
knows-where to be growers themselves with no
further thought of us, only of what they make.

We are all growers left with the knowledge
the farm is not ours, though we are made
of its earth and will again return to it, holy.

                              Mary M. Brown

Roses

After Lawrence Alma-Tadema's *The Roses of Heliogabalus*

As clever as she was in life,
so she remained after death—
my grandmother,
whose ghost one day
for no apparent reason
visited—no, washed over—me
in the checkout line at Kroger,

Her spirit smelling
like every rose
of Eden,
Xanadu,
and Shangri-La,
so overflowing with her favorite scent
that it cascaded over me
as I stood unsuspecting
among racks of tabloids,
bubble gum, and beef jerky,

A floral perfume
flooding my nostrils,
streaming like ribbons
from my fingertips until I felt
as if I had been dipped
and rolled and smothered
in roses,

Almost like the victims
of Heliogabalus,
crazed Roman emperor
with death's gallows written
into his very name,
fabled to have suffocated
his banquet guests beneath

a cataclysm of falling roses
for no reason other than
he could.

But where he
used roses as a weapon,
my grandmother
used them for wisdom,
to show me that,
alive or dead,
there is no time or place,
not even a Tuesday afternoon
at a supermarket,
where she
cannot reach me,
where she cannot wrap
me in love as fragrant and soft
as a rose-scented blanket
for no reason other than
because she can.

Shayla Hawkins

Let Words Out Like Rain

Let words out like rain,
banquets crumble,
kings wander into the wrong ditch.

Let and let and let and there are eyes
in the mountains of god,
backward players hustling each other
at the final table,
a dog who is dying every day
of his goddamn life.

And no one is stopping
or in any way noticing
as the heavens get shot
till they fall onto the hills.

And there is a king inside me
finally emerging,
and I let it develop as it intends,
as the river lets itself go this way and that,
natural along a course already set for it,
or a robin flies off towards new adventure,
blissfully unaware of the arrow that seeks it from afar.

Matt Nagin

Still Life with Bees

In the dim half-light turned blue, she gazes
up at the bees who've trapped themselves
in her skylight, the slow hum of tired wings
beating against fat, desperate bodies.

A lone fly flits about up there, also, at ease
in its unbelonging. The bees circle
in growing anxiety, then slow to a crawl.
My throat tightens as I see my mother

grab the flyswatter. *Don't*, I whisper,
but her tiny frame is already climbing up
on the kitchen table, her focus unwavering.
Oh, I won't kill them, she grins,

her arm extending the fly swatter high,
a meager offering swathed in good cheer.
I rush over to steady her body to keep her
from tipping over in this precarious pursuit.

She waves away my offer to trade places
with her. *You're very pregnant*, she says,
and her tone tells me there is no arguing
with her. My mother murmurs in Mandarin

to the agitated creatures, calling them
beautiful, letting them know she sees them,
sees how they've been up there for far too long
swelling with exhaustion and mistrust.

The first bee slowly climbs onto the swatter
as if entranced by her sweet, clear voice.
She hands me the swatter, and I fumble
with the backyard door, nervously

carrying it into her garden. I place the bee atop
one of my mother's flowerbeds. It clings
to a sunset-orange bud, and I make my way
back inside. In silence, we retrieve, hand off,

and rehome each bee until all eight are
safely in the garden. Not one makes
any move to leave, content to simply rest
a while, to savor the fresh air, to revel

in the sacred space my mother holds
for every being she meets. In the fading light,
I watch her linger in the bare kitchen, a shadow
of a smile gracing her face. If only

they could see her in this light. Would anything
change? Or would she still merely be the next subway
push, another fatal stabbing as she returns home,
one more life snuffed out in a now-empty nail salon?

Melody Wang

Wild Weed Salad

I spy milkweed pods, their seeds cool and damp,
pigweed with a tail filled with little beans to gather,
and dandelions, butter yellow when rubbed on your chin.
Blow white umbrellas into the wind;
in fields, no one cares where seeds land.

Lamb's quarters with fuzzy sage-scented leaves,
mingle with chickweed's little mouse ears.
Purslane blends beautifully with
creeping charlie around the corner.
Violets have come to join their friends—
no one tells them to grow in a straight line.

My favorite, Queen Anne's lace, causes
Creation! Jubilation!
My mind soars with wonder.
I'll make a salad with all that I see,
put their parts together,
trim with care, decorate and make it for me alone.

Weeds grow where they ought to be,
and wildflowers are independent, sprouting up unplanned.
I am so glad they're here to smell, see, and touch,
filling me with magic.
This field brings gifts to my spirit,
peace to my mind,
and solitude and unconditional love
to my soul.

LeAnn Jones

Bud

I spotted her from several blocks away. She was little more than two inches tall, a dark wool coat wrapped so tightly around her she could barely walk. She tottered down the sidewalk with great difficulty, blown this way and that by gusts of wind from the subway grates. As I got closer, I saw that she was not a woman after all, but a young girl of twelve, or perhaps a child of three or four. The coat, a deep verdant green, looked expensive. A viridian silk scarf covered her head and neck and would've covered her face as well had it not slipped, revealing a defiant expression. Just as we were about to pass each other, a large black dog stopped to question her, but before he could take a sniff, she leapt up onto the fender of a parked car and from there, opening wide her wool coat, caught a draft and sailed over the city traffic before disappearing around a corner. The dog looked at me with sad eyes. *She'll be okay*, I said. *She might even grow up to be President one day*. "But I wanted to eat her," whined the dog, whose owner, distracted by a bus that had burst into flames, had no idea what we were talking about.

Peter Anderson

Tabloid

Traffic slows in front of our yard—
a sea of yellow blooms two weeks after
knee-deep snow is news.

Publication continues
until September.
Tulips, irises, lilies
hit the front page.

July is slow,
then gardens release
late fireworks of zinnias.
Echinacea grabs attention
like headlines.

Gladiolas hear gossip,
show off, close out
the summer in style.

Jan Chronister

Elegy for Tropical Houseplants

Tall green plants reach for the skylight
replacing a fig tree our architect gave us.
It died long ago. It's not that death we mourn
but the gloomy crotons, dragon trees, and the ZZ.

They miss Gigi, who watered, pruned, and talked
to them for thirty years, then left us high and dry.
The unemptied washer and dryer were signs
of pique that we pressured her to get vaccinated.

I water the plants every few weeks or whenever
I remember, but I fear for them as one fears
for polar bears on icebergs floating out to sea.

Lois Baer Barr

Listening

I awaken to the sound
of my granddaughter
telling Grandpa
she has seven dollars,
stretching syllables like clay.
She knows I work nights,
this six-year-old girl, and asks
Grandpa when I'm getting up.

Usually, I'm out of bed
at the sound of her feet
tapping wood floors,
ready to read to her,
play a game of Go Fish with her,
or take her for ice cream.

But this evening, as night waltzes
toward us, I want to linger in bed,
listening to the sweet song of her voice.

Robin Wright

Egg Moon, Pink Moon, Sprouting Grass Moon

Everything is blooming,
flowering, leafing
in the middle of the night,
when I become a dream of
a thousand and more petals,
as many branches and roots,
a dream blowing from the sky
of my mind soon as I wake,
yet rooted in the wilderness
of my body. This dawn
as I leave home for work,
I know Earth is dreaming,
imagining my body—
all bodies—
and that the universe
is imagining Earth,
and the full moon above
the flowering cherry tree
is one exquisite petal
blown skyward, suspended in
a single, continuous dream.

Liza Hyatt

Family Tree

Tree of time,
tree of origins,
story tree, spirit tree,
tree of life,
Yggdrasil,
Crann na Beatha,
axis mundi,
sacred grove,
ash and thorn, apple and oak.

The ringed trunk, a door.
Every branch, every leaf, a door.
The doorway to the underworld in the roots.

A tree whose branches stretch over every land.
A tree that survives fire, sword, famine.

A tree whose fruit is every grandmother, every
great-great-as-far-back-as-we-can-go grandmother
who lived to birth babies who lived to birth babies
who lived to birth babies who lived.

A tree that breathes and breathed us into being.

A tree whose exhalations remember
the eukaryotes' eucharist,
the first breath of the first cell with a nucleus,
matter consecrated, life's beginning.

A tree whose boughs become trees themselves.
A tree of trees.
A tree that is a forest,
a forest of tangled paths survived by wandering cousins,
a forest that is a planet,
a planet where everyone is related,
a forest growing out of chaos,
a fractal forest of fractal trees,
the whole within each twig,
each green cell.

Liza Hyatt

Into White

covered hands and head,
swaddled, bound close,
outside in the snow
while Mummy slept.

beside a half-rotten picket fence,
a streetlight's sickly tone-glow
sunk itself into white.

I wanted, tried to sing
as so many times before,
but nothing
save the crunch of boots on white,
and what I hoped for
stuck tight in the throat;
I sniffed your woolen head instead.

in summer months, I carried you on my back
under copper veins and downy birch,
then pausing, like in church, to crane my neck
and see you tucked behind,
staring into white.
all that shock had dammed right up,
let rip.

I dreamt you'd become a naturalist,
wide eyes blending near and far,
then in a blink, set right.

Will Griffith

The Gift

In every memory you wear the same
threadbare sweater. Hem stained
with huckleberries and Pennzoil.
Elbows worn through, then darned,
then worn through again. Giving way
at both shoulders, the seams
leave stitches loose in midair.
The collar is almost severed—
it hovers above the chest
like a necklace. I can mend it,
you'd said, even the mistakes
in the braided cables, knitted by hand
when you were little more
than a boy. Your mother
wanted it to last, I remember
the story going, so the size
was for a future you,
your final height predicted
by an awkward middle school
stage, late adjustments
based on your father's build.
By the time you and I met,
an unraveling cuff exposed
half your forearm's boat tattoo,
the waistband wouldn't stop
riding up and had to be
pulled forever downward.
Your mother's estimates of you
were modest. Not mine.
In my mind you will always be
hunched over a needle, fixing
what was wrong from the start.

Anders Carlson-Wee

Primer

And what if you have nothing?
I pick up a stick. Yes, that's always first.
And next? I see what I can see around me.
Find the sun or moon. Find high ground.
Find north by where the moss grows.
Yes. Now close your eyes. Find them.
The sun's behind. I can feel it
on my neck. High ground's to my right.
North's ahead. Yes. And the wind?
The wind's west. It cools my left temple.
Yes. And next? If I can bug out
I bug out. Otherwise, I go high
and dig a foxhole and tie something bright
above me. You're forgetting something.
Right—first I cut my name in the dirt,
then I go high. Yes. And next?
I walk a loop with my bright thing in sight.
If I find a better stick, I switch for it.
Yes. And if you need to cry?
I crawl inside my foxhole and cry.
And what do you tell yourself as you cry?
Someone's coming. Yes. And what if
no one comes? Each hour I call
in all directions. I listen. Yes.
And what do you listen for?
Sounds that shouldn't be there. Yes.
Sounds that should be there but aren't.
Yes. And what have you heard
since we started? A bird. Yes. Another bird
far away. Yes. A gust in the trees.
Yes. Your voice, if your voice counts.
Yes, my voice counts.

Anders Carlson-Wee

Listening to North in the Morning

I know it's a frittata because last night
we dumpstered a boatload of eggs
and I can hear the tap tap tapping
on the lip of a bowl. I count the cracks
and smile at eighteen because he's breaking
the record. Shuffle of socks on the floor.
A suction gives way to a low whir,
and I know he's in the fridge. Butter
and cheese for sure, but what else
is he rummaging for? Five trips
to the counter before the door sucks shut.
Chopping. Scraping. More Chopping.
The sizzle of the pan reaches me
before the scent of garlic does.
I like listening to him get reckless,
even though half of everything is mine
and I'd never waste so much on one
meal. Isn't that the secret indulgence
of friendship: being near what you
can never be? Now the unoiled
back door, and he's out in the garden.
Rosemary. Wild onion. He's talking
to someone, but who? His laughter
is strong this early in the morning.
Now back in the kitchen making a hard
patter of something: Did he find
that Colombian dark roast I hid
in the bottom drawer? I hope he did.

Anders Carlson-Wee

A Flower (II)

A flower
is a splendidly delicate creation,
and its appearance opens
vibrantly
to wonder, allure, hope.

But the splendor is short-lived,
and eventually
its spell of beauty becomes
only a faded memory.

And yet,
within the flower is
a seed.

Chuck Kellum

The Garden of Us

Restless on a hot full-moon night,
we slip out the back door
down the path to the arched iron gate,
and enter.

Moving past moonflowers surrounding our lily pond,
we follow warmed pine fragrance
to the grove we planted long ago
and stand inhaling the night,
then lie on cool, needle-covered earth to muse.

I remember the time I tripped on a gnarled root,
fell flat, unable to get up
until you came
and wordlessly lay beside me,
put your hand on my back,
and breathed on my neck.

You recall the sultry night
we ran out into the midnight storm,
shed our clothes and danced,
charged with lightning
and fire.

Rising, we approach the raspberry patch
we set out our third year here,
where we'd come on warm mornings
to fill our mouths with sweetness
and laugh as red juice
dripped down our chins.

Now we reach with awareness
through tangled briars
grown thick with thorns and wild with neglect
for hidden fruit still alive here
and savor every precious drop.

Circling back to our bench by the pond,
we sit as clouds block the moon
and water turns inky.

The dark years of illness and loss emerge
when the hope/despair wheel spun endlessly
through our days and nights,
when we took turns falling and sinking,
then rising and leading,
an uncoordinated tandem
without lanterns in the dark.

Until, eventually, we came
to this safe place and rested.

And watched suns and moons and stars
rise and set,
and found our place
in the cycles of the seasons.

These days we come here
to enjoy snapdragon volunteers
with wild vines climbing their stems
alongside flourishing, weedy lavender patches.

Remembering long days working together
cultivating the beautiful and lush,
we smile at an unkemptness
we used to keep in check,
and rest in that which endures.

We give thanks for what we've been given
and bow to what's coming.

Rosanne Megenity Peters

This Poem Has Been Modified

For R. and S.

to fit that blissful moment while falling
asleep, when pain dissipates, you start to lose
all awareness of your legs and feet,
and you feel like those vertical puffs of cloud
whose bottom halves have been erased.

You wake to news of the poet's mountain
of medical bills. Information doesn't take away
pain, offers only circles, dry leaves caught
in a fence, and dreams in which you drive around
to find where you parked the car you are driving.
The *ondes martenot* in the music on the radio
wails, *Where is the way?*

Yet flowers and tree buds are opening, spring rain
contains vitamin B12, and the poet and his wife
continue to care for each other, grateful
for having long ago each chosen someone
who stops to take pictures of tiny flowers.

Meg Freer

Invocation to the Sun: A Yoga Meditation

1

Arms held up, fingers intertwined, body
bending backwards, deep breath:

I'm here, sun, I'm here,
whether in tangled blue bayou,
along Florida's thigh of beach,
Europe's fountain, South American
mountain, California forest clearing:

brown as a beetle-nut,
blond as chamomile,
naked as an eel,
open as a cistern,
shining, freshly minted

I'm everywhere, sun, I'm here.

2

Feet and palms of hands on ground,
deep breath:

I'm low as I can go
and not be flat on my back.
I'm stretching like a rainbow,
head to toe back to ordinary origins:

a tuber planted squat in peat moss,
sweet potatoes and avocado seeds
stuck in pickle and jam jars
lined along the window sill

sprouting thin white filaments.
Both feet on the earth, my head
almost buried in the stuff:
what can I say without my roots?

3

Hands on ground, left leg forward,
right leg thrown back, deep breath:

Does my right hand know
where my left leg takes me
when it puts its best foot forward?

No, it just signs the papers,
shakes the hands that confirm
the coincidences of my footloose ways.

The train can wait, the road can rest:
like my left foot, it's always there.

4

Hands on ground, right leg forward,
left leg thrown back, deep breath:

Does my left hand care
when my right leg bends
tripping love at first sight

wrapped around a smooth warm thigh?
It comes in handy in the acrobatics,
offers support and variation

but never takes part in the creation.
It can't write, can't hitch, can't draw.
All it knows how to do is bitch

and with a flicker of despair
how to cast careless love aside.

5

Hands on ground, feet thrown back,
backside up, head down, deep breath:

I submit, world,
take this shell to hell and back,
I don't care where or how.

I'm a screen of dreams,
an attic of possibilities
where all night I play

dollhouse with shadows
until the real people rise,
life jumps awake and

I submit, world, I submit.

6

Feet back, hands flat on ground, head
tilted up toward the sun, deep breath:

I aspire, strain
up from this net of daily
loss. I hold steady.
Stream-lined.

Maybe lost, maybe misdirected,
maybe not so young and limber,
but sleek and ready as a cobra
shooting straight,
arching high into the sky,
bullseye of the sun.

7

Standing erect, palms pressed together,
deep breath:

The Buddha's on a fishing trip,
Jesus in the deep-freeze,
but I pause now, here to stay:
aware as an astronaut,
determined as a matador,
quiet as a librarian,
calm as a lily pond
where at twilight bullfrogs
croak a chorus to Horus
waiting for the sun to die.

I respire: inhale and exhale,
am my own breath, my own fire.
The breather, the fleshy bellows,
that fellow's somewhere else,

a puff of smoke rising
from these ashes
to be cast upon
the currents of the river.

James Nolan

Dandelions

Every thing will change to a ghost
    of its old self—
The mourning-dove on the fencepost,
    a dusty shelf

In the barn, above the haymow,
    and the windmill,
Turning to rust, and silent now,
    though the wind still

Finds a way through the broken vanes.
    Not for long, all
That has changed, and is pale. That wanes,
    like the dove's call.

Jared Carter

Blackberry Leaves

Blackberry leaves slip their flavors
into autumn in memory of fruit ripening,
to have me remember the blackberries
and my sons gathering.

Turning slowly through bramble corridors,
the flat heat already thick and layered
on this morning of late July,
the three of us behold,
with proper lift of thorn, untouched clusters,
the essence of what sun can turn with darkness.

Picking, dropping the fruit into our pails,
we watch the stains of our fingertips darken,
leaving words, like the green berries,
for later, for remembering
with the colors of these leaves now,
how are palms turned upward, how our pails filled.

Stephen R. Roberts

Bent Cows

The cows are bent again.
It's tough on the cud-chewers,
the way the wind blows here,
crosswise and cataclysmic.
Come morning, it'll be easy
enough to tie them fast
to a double-braced corner post
and crank them out straight
again with the tractor winch.
Like muscling a coat hanger
into a flamingo lawn bird,
there's a semblance of deranged,
compromised beauty in it.
Through the entire process,
the cows remain cooperative.
They're such likable beasts
if you care for laid-back
and dull-witted.
Though I'm not so sure
about the dull-witted.
That's easy to confuse
with bovine meditations
or prayer hour down
at the cattle-crossing.
The way they're settled
into themselves—that gold
sparkle in the slow eye—
makes me wonder
if they have answers
to our financial crisis,
global warming,
and how to end the wars
by milking time.

Stephen R. Roberts

124

Male Pattern

It creeps back from either
side like a meandering
river trying to cut off
the widow's peak of
peninsula and turn
it into an oxbow island.

I watch it recede in
glacial desperation, knowing
that the forces at
work here are generations
old and as implacable
as a code-carved double helix.

So, rather than stare my
own denuded hairline in
the eye, I hide it with the
expedient camouflage
of razor and cream
and pretend it's my own
choice to shine a little
too brightly in direct sunlight,
and not a masked pattern of
testosterone-driven deforestation.

Chris Hasara

Education

I spent three weeks
one spring
learning how to swing
a mattock because
we couldn't afford a rototiller
for my dad's garden.

I easily taught myself the right technique
(not wanting to shorten
a foot by a few toes is a great
educational motivator),
but spent the rest of
the time learning that I
hate working without a shirt—
flying dirt sticks to sun-
watered skin.
I learned that I had strength
enough to work for an hour or more
at a time, but focus enough for
twenty minutes tops before I was
liable to get lost in dangerous daydreams.
I learned that I liked the feel
of the sweat-smoothed wood sliding
through my hand with every tilling
blow and the way callouses
formed to protect me
from my overzealous grip.

Chris Hasara

Wind

Wicked wailing winds
shriek,
throwing rain,
hitting windows
like wild animals
clawing at fragile glass.

Judy Young

Sheep Shearing Time

Sitting on the edge of the bluff
under tall sighing pines
swaying, whispering
to gentle breezes,
caressing their long needles.
Green pastures slope,
flowing to the woods.
Gray clouds roll into skeins,
mimicking woolen piles
from the shearing
as they run
over bleating sheep
standing naked
in the shed pens.

Judy Young

127

Growth

see the garden ...
the cat enters in
with a movement
reminiscent
of bigger kin ...

see the garden ...
citronella scents
down insects
with fatal fragrance ...
exoskeletons frozen
in waxen coffins ...

see the garden ...
the cat enters in ...
the rodent then
gingerly taken
along a woven
course among
growth & stem ...
its popping eyes ...
its dangling tongue ...

see the garden ...
the sated kitten ...
the dying flame ...
the thickening dim ...
the curious flies ...

See the garden.

J. T. Whitehead

Roots

Forest fires are natural.
Most of the time.

I cast a lit cigarette
into the pile of kindling
I had so carelessly organized.
The flame started slowly
but grew,
glowing, illuminating my face.
Soon I was working to guide
the flames,
walling myself off from the world—
my scorched kingdom

Rain began to fall,
quenching the flames.
Far be it for me to fan them further—
Mother Nature has spoken.
I settle into this valley of death
I have orchestrated.

Sleep comes violent and aggressive.
A necessary distraction.
My bed made of
soot and ash is
a fitting domicile
for a man like me.

A single seed flits on a breeze,
traveling from its home atop the mountain
Toward a column of smoke.
Luckily, the winds change,
carrying the seed away from danger.

It lands on the shore of a gentle brook.
Water is abundant,
but there is no soil,
no loam to provide a
safe home to sprout.

So it waits for a bird—
some creature, anything—
to change its destiny.

I am awoken by a tender caress.
I brush my cheek
and find against it a
sycamore seedling,
something so insignificant that
would have previously been trodden underfoot
without acknowledgment.
It seems so precious to me now.
Something green in this
sea of charcoal.

I plunge my thumb into the ground
and place my hopes into that
dark, rich soil,
praying it will take root.

Matthew Whybrew

She Watches the Sky

In the morning
while it is still raining,
she steps out of our hogan,
looks toward the morning
and around back
to the disappearing night.
It is time.

Amá sání wakes her young.
It is time to play in the earth,
time for the story, and
time to plant three sisters
in the storm-softened arroyo—
one to grow strong and tall,
one to climb
looking over these mountains,
one to stay low,
covering the ground.

By high sun,
we are done,
gathered back to shade,
washing mud from hands and
smiling faces.

Summer will burn,
cracking the earth dry,
but at its end,
the three sisters
will offer themselves
as maize, tepari, and squash
to weather the cold season
as it approaches.

Amá sání puts her young to sleep,
looks toward the darkness growing,
looks back toward the setting day,
knowing quiet of days ahead
as she reads it across the sky.

Michael E. Strosahl

The finch, the thistle
cycle of propagation
song of flight and thorns

In the act of death
my seed falls to fertile soil
soul's eternal bloom

John Hinton

Bees prepare the stage
summer sashays in
bringing naked ladies

The climbing tree
summer day at Grandma's
trying not to break a bone

Mary Hinton

Seeking Stones

On the first nice day of spring
when the sun is shining and
the breeze wafts fresh,
I go to the cemetery and
seek out the weathered stones—
the ones on which no names can be read.

I place paper to the stone,
lightly rubbing chalk across the surface in
an attempt to pull forth an impression.
I'm not sure if I'm trying to know them somehow,
or attempting to bring the dead to life.

On this day, a singular word, "Baby."
No name, no dates.
I am threatened by grief,
captured by anger.
Did the parents not care enough to assign a name?

The bright day darkens dreary and
birds' chatter ceases.
I am offended by indifference.
I want to sob and rage.
What kind of people were this mother/father?
Both were undeserving of such titles.

I feel a hand on my shoulder,
light and small,
a contrast to my emotional turmoil.
A child's voice speaks:
"They, too, were threatened by grief,
captured by anger."

John R. Hinton

Striving for Light

Raking wet winter leaves from my lawn,
cold's grip on inclemency loosening,
spring's commencing clasp tightening,
allowing the warm, soothing palm of Mother Nature.

Amid decaying brown and burgeoning green,
a fragile flower
causes me to pause and contemplate
the contentiousness of the crocus.

Not to warmth, but in warming it rises,
thrusting a tender head through algid ground,
breaching a blanket of snow,
stubbornly striving for light.

I marvel at the fury of such a delicate thing,
astonished at my thoughts
as I am usually resigned
to allow winter to reside in my soul.

I return to my raking,
careful to maneuver around the blossom,
thankful for this reminder of my own resilience—
a lesson taught by a frangible, determined bloom.

John R. Hinton

Delaware Bay Reunion

I dragged my former roommate Brian to watch the migrant sandpipers assembled for horseshoe crab spawning. Though it was June and the years of overharvesting crabs had started, we still found crowds of Red Knots and Ruddy Turnstones, which Brian, a word-botcher, decided were called runny turdstones. Both rust-black-and-white, the knots are brush-stroked and the turnstones are stenciled by a car-customizer—you should look them up. A few Semipalmated Plovers scurried from bug to bug. And all along the sand were horseshoe crabs, creeping seemingly at random or wrecked and desiccated, their moving parts exposed. Their iron-gray roe lay in swaths and swales.

> The same eggs over and over,
> the same birds. Doesn't the tide
> wash the piper and plover
> shit to where algae ride?

As we walked through the flocks, the birds leaving bubbles of space around us, I couldn't resist learning what they were tasting. I pinched up a few eggs and lipped them in. Brian said, "Jerry!" I grinned, strode on, and didn't say, "What's the problem?" I'd hardly partaken as luridly as when Galway Kinnell ate bloody droppings of the bear he was tracking. The difference is that I really did it. Sorry, that's unfair to you. Anyway, I presume I'm too old to publicly put whatever in my mouth. Are you also? The eggs were salty and sour; you're missing nothing but a boast of abasement.

King Canute gormandized on Red Knots fattened with bread and milk, legend says. Like its namesake, *Calidris canutus* cannot hold off the waves, but we may be creeping between greed and need.

Gerald Friedman

The Curé d'Ars, Saint Jean Marie Baptiste Vianney: A Triptych

I. The Left Panel, Une Taverne à Ars

In the smoky dimness of a tavern
some village men sit with their pipes
and clay cups of bitter wine.
Like their oxen, now in their stalls,
relieved of their yokes and goads,
they are at ease beside others
who also suffer heavy loads.
"Monsieur le Curé, he has banished the dances.
My daughters, les jeunes femmes, cry all day.
'I cannot be with Pierre,'
'I cannot dance with Henri,'
or wear their ribbons and frills.
They cannot show their arms or pretty necks.
They are pretty for just so long."
"Monsieur le Curé will banish your tavern, Bernard."
"Bah! Did not Jesus make wine at Cana?"
"Mais pas cette pisse du diable, Bernard."
"Shut your tongue, Servas. As the Curé says
your mouth is a sewer from hell."
"Monsieur le Curé says we should pray to Our Lady,"
said Coustance and blessed himself.
"Pray that she come here and taste your wine.
'Mon Dieux,' she will say and call her son,"
blessing himself again.
"She will say to him, 'Monsieur Bernard has no wine.'
Our Lord," he blessed himself,
"will tell you to fill a cask with our foul water
and, Voila! Vin d'Avignon! Vin du Pape!"
The men roared with laughter,
drained their cups, and stared at the hearth fire,
which made their shoulders and arms more massive
and darkened the lines of their faces.

II. Center Panel, La Maison de Saint Curé

Before an icon of the Sacred Heart of Jesus—
the flaming, pierced heart, bound with a crown of thorns,
intensified in the light of a small votive lamp—
stands Pere Jean-Marie Baptiste Vianney, the Curé of Ars,
in a linen smock down to his loins,
in his hand, a multi-stranded flail with metal tips.
He prays,
"My Lord, you banished us to this place of exile
 to force us not to be attached to anything in it,"
and whips the flail over his shoulder.
"Our bodies are vessels of corruption,"
and flails again.
"And are meant for death,"
and flails himself again,
"Are meant for the worms and nothing more,"
and flails again.
"My Savior, I accept all the pains that in your pleasure
you place upon me."
The metal tips dig again into his back.
"I kiss your cross and submit to mine."
The flail sings again.
"The young people and their parents, my flock,
gather at dances," the flail flies,
"where so many sins of impurity are committed."
The iron tips bite his back again.
"There, wordly young women
in their flamboyant attire,"
whoosh the flail flies,
"enflame the hearts of young men,"
the tips now pull at his skin,
"with the fire of concupiscence."
He leans his back against the wall
and slides to the floor
where he will sleep
as he has given his mattress away.
He whispers, "My people, I paid for you."

III. The Right Panel: Sanctuaire d'Arts

The first penitents came fearful for their souls
and of the fiend's fires le Curé had preached,
few at first, then those from nearby villages
where the fears of those fires were already raging
and tales of this herald of God's anger
and of the Curé's absolving cure had spread,
this confessor who could untomb even hidden sins.
After dancing was banished, then the taverns,
it is said the Curé began hearing the sins
of the fear-driven penitents at 1:00 AM
and that 100,000, some said 300,000,
came in a year to the small chapel
in this simple village, today a sanctuary city devoted to
Saint Jean Marie Baptiste Vianney
with a basilica where the Curé's incorrupt body
lies in a glass-topped coffin,
the face a wax mask reflecting his weary serenity,
and La Maison de Saint Curé
preserved as he had left it with his bed he never slept in
that the Devil had set aflame,
and his few possessions but not his barbed flail,
a youthful folly he had called it.
Then there is La Chappelle du Coeur,
the shrine of the Curé's heart,
removed from his incorrupt body,
now proclaimed in a gold reliquary
illumed by hundreds of votive lamps
which make the heart seem to pulsate.
If you have time to continue your pilgrimage
after Ars, you might visit Via Carritas vinyards
established by Pope Clement V in 1309,
just two hundred and sixty-five kilometers south via A7.
There, the Monks of the Benedictine Abbey
of Le Barroux have shouldered the hard work
of cultivating the grapes on the steep slopes of Mont Vertoux.
I recommend their Vox Angelorum
or their Pax in Terra.

John D. Groppe

Interview with John D. Groppe, winner of the Editor's Choice Award for Issue #7

I was born in New York City, but since 1962 I have been a resident of Rensselaer, Indiana, a town of 5800 in a county of 34,000. I was a bona fide New Yorker. I attended the College of the City of New York, and after military service at Fort Benning, Georgia, I spent a year getting an MA in American Literature at Columbia. My plan then was to become a high school English teacher. By the time I completed the MA, the baby boomers were exploding college enrollment records, and I found myself more employable than I thought I was. I taught at Villanova, then part-time as a TA at Notre Dame and later at IU-South Bend. Finally, in 1962, I was hired at a small Catholic College—Saint Joseph's College—in Rensselaer—a town named for another wandering New Yorker. My wife and I had just married and had no idea or plan that we would spend the rest of our lives here.

The college and the town were fruitful places to test Thoreau's quip to Emerson, "I have traveled extensively in Concord." Even though J. Hillis Miller wrote that new criticism had died in 1953, I found that no one at St. Joseph's had yet heard of it, nor had many of my colleagues or professors at Notre Dame or Columbia. At St. Joe's, I had the opportunity right away to teach genre courses—the novel, introduction to poetry, and introduction to drama, but also world literature and, of course, freshman composition—all great opportunities for a young man in love with words, literary forms, and argumentation, and with a flare for the dramatic. My literary experience expanded immediately as I also taught world literature (remember the Norton Anthology?). The faculty of the college was small, so there was much interaction among the faculty of nearly all disciplines and among both clergy and lay. In 1969, St. Joe's adopted an integrated, general education program that challenged me to help both my students and myself to connect a wide variety of human history and culture. Over my teaching career of forty-one years, I taught feature writing, argumentative writing, poetry writing, a writing course for prospective so-called language arts teachers, and always a basic composition course, which was constantly a learning experience in trying to find new ways to push Sisyphus' rock over the ridge of the hill.

Here in Rensselaer, my wife, Rose Marie, and I gave birth to and raised five children and became more fully involved in the town through the children's activities as well as through our own involvement in church, other local organizations, and politics. One aspect of a small town that I found stimulating is that not only are the schools, churches, and shops nearby, but everything is compressed, and you encounter the mayor or city councilmen or state representative or a congressman or senator or the Bishop nearby. In some such towns, one can catch a glimpse of the macrocosm in the microcosm. It's not quite Blake's "a world in a grain of sand," but many small towns have more complexity and diversity than meets the eye. I became involved in a local arts group through my interest in photography and a local writers group that produced fourteen annual anthologies of our writings. I was also active in an arts council that made funds available to bring poets to town. I established The Midwest Poetry Circuit and managed it for about five years. The circuit was a collaboration of small colleges to bring poets to read on their campuses by sharing expenses.

As I age, my geography continues to shrink. Chicago, Indianapolis, and New York are much further away than they once were. Nonetheless, I am still traveling extensively here in my Concord, although I do not encounter as many people doing penance as Thoreau claims he did in Concord.

Does where are you living color your poetry?

I am not a local colorist. My interest in birds led to my collection of poems entitled *The Raid of the Grackles and Other Poems*, and that interest was surely sparked by the opportunity I had here to see more birds and a greater variety of them than I had seen in New York. Yet the title poem of that collection owes as much to the grackles I have seen here at my feeder as to New York street gangs in their dark clothes and shiny, oily hair. The second emerges through the first. To the extent that I can identify the sources of my poetry, I would say that my poems are the result of a fusion of specific local experiences reflected through readings of a wide variety of materials.

How long have you been writing creatively?

I started writing short stories in college and continued into the 70s. In 1969 one of my stories, "A Shred of Decency," was cited by "The Yearbook of the American Short Story" in *Best Short Stories of 1969* as a distinguished story of the year. I guess I found the demands of writing short stories too great to manage along with my teaching, administrative responsibilities, and academic writings, and so I switched to poetry. However, I think I still think as a story writer, and my poems are often stories in capsule. My Caravaggio poem is one such story and was derived from a book, *Caravaggio: The Artist and His Work* by Sybille Ebert-Schifferer.

142

What is a style or genre of poetry or prose that you admire but haven't tried to write?

I wish I could manage blank verse or rhymed verse as I appreciate how rhyme and meter create a dynamic of their own by adding other dimensions to the language and imagery of a poem. I try to substitute experiments with syntax and astute word choices for what I lack in other resources.

Do you have any advice for writers?

I always encourage students and poetry friends to read a wide variety of poetry and to read poems—others and their own—aloud so that they can feel the heft and momentum of the words. I also encourage them to hear recordings of poetry, whether the readings are done by the authors or others. Finally, I would encourage writers to purchase and study a good introduction to poetry book, my favorite being *Western Wind: An Introduction to Poetry* by John Frederick Nims. The book is a good example of a new critical approach to the teaching of poetry. It should be noted that many of the new critics were poets or novelists or short story writers. John Nims was a distinguished poet, and in his introduction to poetry, he wanted to introduce people to poetry from a poet's perspective, from the inside. The book is not a manual. It is an attempt to show some of the many resources that a wide range of poets have used to bring their poems to fruition. Finally, I encourage writers to share their poetry with others and to ask for the readers' sense of their work, but not an immediate response. The readers should have a chance to savor the poems, to live with them for a while, so as to begin to intuit the whole poem and how it fits together, how it works, and only then to comment.

Interview with Mary A. Couch, winner of the Editor's Choice Award for Issue #8

Mary A. Couch was born in Chicago, Illinois and moved to Noblesville, Indiana at the age of seven. She graduated from Noblesville High School, and has work in the food industry, loan and mortgage companies, and telephone answering service. At present she is a part-time Administrative Assistant for Taylored Systems, LLC, a technology company in Noblesville. She learned the art of poetry from her mother and two grandmothers who were storytellers and artists. While working for the telephone answering service, she would take her mother and grandmother to the Broad Ripple Poetry Club and began to share her poetry. Soon, she joined the Noblesville Writers Group where she showed a flair for taking simple everyday objects and turning them into something horrendous by creating unique worlds in her short stories. She then began to join her mom at the Anderson Poetry Corner where she learned different forms of poetry from President Glenna Glee. At this time, Glenna encouraged her to enter National and State contests and become a member of the ISFPC (Indiana State Federation of Poetry Clubs), now PSI (Poetry Society of Indiana). She and her mother would attend the Spring and Fall Rendezvous Meetings, and she served in several capacities as Manningham Chair, Secretary, and was elected Premier Poet, which was the hardest thing to do as she was shy and found it difficult to get up in front of people to read her poems.

She enjoys writing poems showing her Celtic heritage by revealing the spirits that live in nature and the oneness of the universe. Her poems have been published in *"Poetic Nature in the Hoosierland," Twin Muses: Art & Poetry", "An Evening with the Writing Muse," "Polk Street Review," "Encore," "Pegasus," "Poetry and Paint,"* and, with her mother, published a collection of poetry called *"Two Views."* She has published three books, all available on Amazon: *"Hoosier Haiku: Snippets from the Hoosierland," Hoosier WordArt: Communing with the Chippewa,"* and *"Hoosier WordArt: Generations,"* a memorial collection of her mother, Alice Couch's, poetry along with her own.

Where are you living? Does that color your poetry?

I live in Noblesville, Indiana, Hamilton County the Heartland of Indiana. Since I write mostly about nature, I would say somewhat due to the beautiful local and state parks, and also for the rich heritage or history of Hamilton County.

What is your ideal location for writing?

I've been writing since high school, where I could be found during study hall either reading or writing verse. Now, I can pretty much write anywhere—at work if the mood hits me, at home in a chair with my dog, riding in a car, while dining, or just sitting in nature.

Which is your personal favorite of your own poems?

This poem was written for my mother's passing and shares my opinion that when we die it is merely another transition from this life to another. It is but a journey that continues, and we can feel their presence still whether in a memory, a song, the whisper of wind, each reminds us of those who have gone from this time and place. Life is but energy within a shell, and when the shell is gone, the energy is freed to travel on.

Within the Stillness

This essence which you knew as mine has journeyed on,
yet you will encounter me within night's stillness.
I'll be the whispering wind caressing your hair,
or soft tapping of raindrops on your windowpane.
You will see me in the oak tree's autumn splendor,
and hear my voice chirp along with the cricket's song.

I will stroll with you down woodland paths in the sun,
a wisp of memory that brings a smile to your lips.
Within frozen winter's ivory snowflake's, I'll come
bringing an afterglow of happiness to you.

You will hear me in our children's laughter each day,
and your tears will become petals blown by the wind.
I will be gentle notes within those words you read
from my letters and poems beneath the starlight.

You will sense me when you awake in morning's hush,
a familiar presence who lived and enjoyed life.
My memory will wrap you within its strong arms
and you will know, I did not die; I journeyed on.

What is a style or genre of poetry or prose that you admire but haven't tried to write?

The sonnet is an ideal fourteen-line poem, but I have yet to master the correct rhythm (the iambic pentameter) of its form.

What is something surprising about yourself that may not be easily perceived through your writing?

I prefer writing humorous poetry, yet most of my poems that win contests are more serious, instead. I enjoy doing a twist in a poem now and then to surprise the reader.

Do you have any advice for writers?

Write every day. Look at book titles, newspaper headlines, or a line in a story, choose two or three words, and write something. It may be good or bad, but the more you practice writing the better you will get. Challenge yourself to learn a form or style of poetry. You will find it rewarding, and it helps if you enter contests. I started out writing rhyme, yet now I do free verse, haiku, villanelle, pantoum, cinquain, acrostic, limerick, narrative, and several other types of poetry. My favorite forms are the syllabic ones, which is why I enjoy writing traditional haiku the most for its concise format of only three lines and seventeen syllables. I post these on my Facebook page. Short poems are best as they ask you to find precise wording, giving the poem a richer feel and imagery.

David Allen is a retired journalist living in central Indiana. His poems have been published in many journals and anthologies. He is a member and past vice president of the Poetry Society of Indiana. He has four books available from Amazon online at: tinyurl.com/davidallenpoet. Visit his poetry blog at www.davidallen.nu.

Muntather Alsawad was born in Basra, Iraq, where he studied literary criticism and published poetry and criticism of his own. He has lived in Portland, Maine since arriving in the US, and works at the Portland Museum of Art.

George Amabile has published twelve books and has had work in over a hundred national and international venues, including *The New Yorker,*  *Poetry (Chicago), American Poetry Review, Botteghe Oscure, The Globe and Mail, The Penguin Book of Canadian Verse, Saturday Night, Poetry Australia, Sur* (Buenos Aires), *Poetry Canada Review,* and *Canadian Literature.* His most recent publications are a long poem, *Dancing, with Mirrors* (Porcupine's Quill, 2011), *Small Change* (Fiction, Libros Libertad, 2011) and *Martial Music* (poetry, Signature Editions, 2016) all of which have won the prestigious Bressani Award, and an International Crime novel, *Operation Stealth Seed* (Signature Editions, 2019) which won the Michael von Rooy award for genre fiction.

Poet, performer, and playwright **Peter Anderson** grew up outside Detroit and now lives in Vancouver, Canada. His work has appeared or is forthcoming in *Unbroken, Sublunary Review,* the *American Journal of Poetry, Flora Fiction, Thieving Magpie, Rat's Ass Review, Duality, MoonPark Review, Best Microfictions 2022,* and others.

Michael Ansara spent many years as an activist and an organizer. He is the co-founder of Mass Poetry. He currently serves on the Executive Committee of the Redress Movement and the organizing team for Together We Elect. His poems and essays have been published in *Salamander, Mid America Poetry Review, Web del Sol, Ibbetson Street, Glint Literary Review, Euphony, Pine Hills Review, Vox, Solstice,* and *Arrowsmith.* His first book of poems, *What Remains,* will be published next summer by Kelsay Press. He lives in Carlisle, Massachusetts.

Lois Baer Barr lives in Riverwoods, Illinois with her husband and
 golden doodle puppy. Poetry always comes before
watering plants. She has two published chapbooks and
one forthcoming. *Biopoesis* won Poetica's first prize in
2013. *Lope de Vega's Daughter*, flash fiction, is
available at Red Bird Press, and *Tracks: Poems on the
"L"* will be published at Finishing Line Press where it
placed fourth in the New Voices Contest. Her website is
loisbaerbarr.com You can check out *Lope de Vega's Daughter* at
https://www.redbirdchapbooks.com/content/lope-de-vegas-daughter

Mandy Beattie frequently finds herself lost in poetry, books &
imaginings. Pen, paper & words without borders are some of her
favourite things. She has been published in poetry journals such as *Poets
Republic, Wordpeace, Dreich, Last Stanza Poetry Journal*, and
Lothlorien Poetry. She was recently shortlisted in the Black Box
Competition.

Joe Benevento's poems, stories, essays and reviews have appeared in
close to 300 places, including: *Prairie Schooner,
Poets & Writers, Bilingual Review, Cold Mountain
Review,* and *I-70 Review.* Among his fourteen books
of poetry and fiction are *The Odd Squad,* an urban
YA novel, which was a finalist for the 2006 John
Gardner Fiction Book Award, and *Expecting
Songbirds: Selected Poems, 1983-2015,* with the
Purple Flag imprint of the Visual Artists Collective
out of Chicago. Benevento teaches creative writing and American lit.,
including Latinx, at Truman State, where he also serves as poetry editor
for the *Green Hills Literary Lantern.*

Mark Blickley grew up within walking distance of New York's Bronx
Zoo. He is a proud member of the Dramatists Guild and PEN American
Center. His latest book is the flash fiction collection, *Hunger
Pains* (Buttonhook Press).

Ann Work Borger of Indianapolis began writing poetry in mid-life
 while she lived in eastern Pennsylvania. Her chapbook,
Sailing into Sunset, includes poems first published in
Feelings, Writer's Digest, and the PPS Annual chapbook of
contest winners. Since returning to her Indiana roots, she is
a member of PSI. Three of her poems were accepted for inclusion in
INverse, the Indiana Poetry database (2019).

Poems by **Jonathan Bracker** have appeared in *The New Yorker, Poetry Northwest, Southern Poetry Review,* and other periodicals, and in eight collections, the latest of which, from Seven Kitchens Press, is *Attending Junior High.*

A retired writing professor, **Mary M. Brown** lives in Anderson, Indiana. Her work appears on the Poetry Foundation and American Life in Poetry websites and recently in *Rockvale Review, Thimble, Open: Journal of Arts and Letters,* and in *New Poetry from the Midwest.* She is the poetry editor of *Flying Island.*

Michael H. Brownstein has been widely published throughout the small and literary presses. His work has appeared in *The Café Review, American Letters and Commentary, Skidrow Penthouse, Xavier Review, Hotel Amerika, Free Lunch, Meridian Anthology of Contemporary Poetry, The Pacific Review, Poetrysuperhighway.com* and others. In addition, he has nine poetry chapbooks including *The Shooting Gallery* (Samidat Press, 1987), *Poems from the Body Bag* (Ommation Press, 1988), *A Period of Trees* (Snark Press, 2004), *What Stone Is* (Fractal Edge Press, 2005), *I Was a Teacher Once* (Ten Page Press, 2011) and *Firestorm: A Rendering of Torah* (Camel Saloon Press, 2012). His latest volumes of poetry, *A Slipknot to Somewhere Else* (2018) and *How Do We Create Love?* (2019), were recently released (Cholla Needles Press).

Roger Camp lives in Seal Beach, CA where he tends his orchids, walks the pier, plays blues piano, and spends afternoons with his pal, Harry, over drinks at Saint & 2nd. When he's not at home, he's traveling in the Old World. His work has appeared in *American Journal of Poetry, North American Review, Gulf Coast, Southern Poetry Review,* and *Nimrod.*

Lorraine Caputo is a documentary poet, translator, and travel writer. Her works appear in over 300 journals on six continents and 20 collections of poetry, including *On Galápagos Shores* (dancing girl press, 2019) and *Caribbean Interludes* (Origami Poems Project, 2022). She also authors travel narratives, articles, and guidebooks. Her writing has been honored by the Parliamentary Poet Laureate of Canada (2011) and nominated for the Best of the Net. Caputo has given literary readings from Alaska to the Patagonia. She journeys through Latin America, listening to the voices of the pueblos and Earth. More at: latinamericawanderer.wordpress.com

Envy Cardena is an Indigenous poet who is passionate about Indigenous activism and mental health awareness. Raised on an American Indian reservation, their bloodline includes Eastern Band Cherokee (enrolled) and Oglala Lakota. Viewing the world through Indigenous eyes, Envy is influenced by gothic literature and music, pop culture, and their own cultural practices.

Anders Carlson-Wee is the author of *The Low Passions* (W.W. Norton, 2019), a New York Public Library Book Group Selection. His work has appeared in *The Paris Review, BuzzFeed, Ploughshares, VQR, Harvard Review, The Sun, The Southern Review*, and *The Best American Nonrequired Reading*. The recipient of fellowships from the National Endowment for the Arts, Poets & Writers, Bread Loaf, Sewanee, and the Napa Valley Writers' Conference, he is the winner of the Poetry International Prize. His work has been translated into Chinese. Anders holds an MFA from Vanderbilt University and is represented by Massie & McQuilkin Literary Agents. www.anderscarlsonwee.com

Dan Carpenter is an Indianapolis freelance writer who has published poems and stories in many journals, along with two books of poems, *The Art He'd Sell for Love* (Cherry Grove, 2015) and *More Than I Could See* (Restoration, 2009).

Jared Carter's seventh collection of poems, *The Land Itself,* is from Monongahela Books in West Virginia. He lives in Indianapolis.

Alys Caviness-Gober is an anthropologist, artist, and writer. Despite lifelong disabilities, she perseveres with art and nonprofit volunteering. Alys taught Anthropology, Women's Studies, and ESOL at the university level, and was a PhD candidate in Applied Linguistics until her disabilities worsened in 2009. Alys and author Sarah E. Morin are the cofounders of the literature-based annual project *Noblesville Interdisciplinary Creativity Expo* (NICE). In November 2014, Alys founded *Logan Street Sanctuary, Inc.* (LSS), an all-volunteer 501(c)(3) Arts organization and the organization took over hosting the annual *Noblesville Interdisciplinary Creativity Expo* (NICE) project and the publication of the annual anthology *The Polk Street Review*. In July 2019, LSS rebranded as *Community • Education • Arts* (CEArts); Alys serves as the President of *CEArts*. She is a selected poet for *INverse: Indiana's Poetry Archive*, and a member of both *Noble Poets* and the *Poetry Society of Indiana*. Alys' poetry has been featured in global anthologies since the 1980s, in the *Last Stanza Poetry Journal, The Polk Street Review*, and in her own poetry and artwork collections, *Naked In*

Wonderland (Volumes I, II, III, IV). She serves on the *Noblesville Cultural Arts Council* and is active in the local arts scene. Alys' artwork, photographs, and poetry have received national and international recognition.

Jan Chronister writes in the woods near Maple, Wisconsin and is waiting for her yard to begin the annual parade of blooms. Jan is the author of two full-length poetry collections and five chapbooks.

Jeffrey Clapp's poems, stories and translations have appeared in Samovar, North American Review, Blue Unicorn, Dalhousie Review, Arkansas Review, Sycamore Review and many others. He is a past recipient of the Daniel Morin Poetry Prize at UNH and the Indiana Fiction Prize from Purdue. His work has been anthologized in *Best of Blueline* and *Like Thunder: Poets Respond to Violence in America.* He currently lives in South Portland, Maine.

W.B. Cornwell is an award-winning poet, novelist, genealogy blogger, and half of the writing team known as Storm Sandlin. He is a member of Last Stanza Poetry Association. In 2016, Ben and his cousin A.N. Williams organized the campaign for Elwood, Indiana's Poetry Month. He is a featured writer for Goodkin.org and is currently working on a slew of writing projects, including various charity publications, co-authorships, and screenplays. Cornwell is a husband and father.

Mary A. Couch, an Administrative Assistant for Taylored Systems LLC, a technology company in Noblesville, learned the art of poetry from her mother, and two grandmothers who were storytellers and artists. She enjoys writing poems showing her Celtic heritage by revealing the spirits that live in nature and the oneness of the universe. Her poems have been published in a variety of venues, including *Poetic Nature in the Hoosierland, Twin Muses: Art & Poetry, An Evening with the Writing Muse, Polk Street Review, Encore, Pegasus, and Poetry and Paint.* She is a published author on Amazon with three books: *Hoosier Haiku: Poetic Snippets from the Heartland—Hoosier WordArt: Communing with the Chippewa,* and *Hoosier WordArt: Generations.* She and her mother also published a chapbook called *Two Views.* She is a past Premier Poet for the Poetry Society of Indiana. She won the Editor's Choice award for this issue of *Last Stanza Poetry Journal.*

Featured artist **Laura Crawford** paints in acrylics—vibrantly colored scenes from nature: rolling landscapes, flowing cloudscapes, mountains, trees, gardens, and flowers. The  unifying theme is flow and change. Each scene is fleeting and captures a moment, and her hope is that this sense of fleeting beauty inspires mindfulness, appreciating and celebrating these moments when they occur. Laura comes from a family of painters. In addition to their modeling, teaching, and inspiration, she has had off-and-on formal art training. She is a full-time artist in Broad Ripple Village in Indianapolis with her beloved sculptor husband and their old, bossy cat. Laura's portfolio can be seen on her web site: laura-crawford.com.

Sandra de Helen's essays and poetry appear in *Artemis Journal, Dramatist, ROAR, The Medical Journal of Australia, The Dandelion Review, Lavender Review, Sweatpants & Coffee, Mom Egg*, and other journals. Her full-length poetry collections (*Desire Returns for a Visit,* 2018*, Lesbian Humor is Not an Oxymoron,* 2019*, Poetry for the People,* 2020, and *The World's a Stage,* 2021) are published by Launch Point Press.

Among **Karl Elder**'s honors are the Christopher Latham Sholes Award from the Council for Wisconsin Writers; a Pushcart  Prize; the Chad Walsh, Lorine Niedecker, and Lucien Stryk Awards; and two appearances in *The Best American Poetry*. His novel, *Earth as It Is in Heaven*, is from Pebblebrook Press. Both *Alpha Images: Poems Selected and New* (Water's Edge Press) and *Reverie's Ilk: Collected Prose Poems* (Cyberwit) appeared in 2020.

Meg Freer grew up in Montana and lives in Ontario, where she enjoys the outdoors year-round. She works as an editor and teaches piano. She  has co-authored a chapbook, *Serve the Sorrowing World with Joy* (Woodpecker Lane Press, 2020). Her photos, poetry and prose have been published in anthologies and journals such as *Arc Poetry, Queen's Quarterly, The Sunlight Press, Eastern Iowa Review, Sequestrum*, and *Ruminate*.

Gerald Friedman grew up in the suburbs of Cleveland, Ohio, and now teaches physics and math in Santa Fe, New Mexico. He has published poems in various journals, recently *Better Than Starbucks, As It Ought To Be, Rat's Ass Review*. You can read more of his work at https://jerryfriedman.wixsite.com/my-site-2

Mary Ardeth Gaylord was a poet and librarian who spent most of her adult life in Indiana. Mary was a brave, humorous, and deeply religious woman. She passed away in 2020; her joyous, generous spirit is greatly missed by all who loved her and lives on in her poetry.

Timothy Geiger is the author of the poetry collection *Weatherbox*, winner of the 2019 Vern Rutsala Poetry Prize from Cloudbank Books.

 He has also published the full-length collections, *The Curse of Pheromones* (Main Street Rag) and *Blue Light Factory* (Spoon River Poetry Press) and ten chapbooks, most recently, *Holler* (APoGee Press). His work has been the recipient of a Pushcart Prize XVII, a Holt, Rinehart and Winston Award in Literature, and many state and local grants in Alabama, Minnesota, and Ohio. He is also the proprietor of the literary fine-press Aureole Press at the University of Toledo, where he teaches creative writing, poetry, and book arts.

James Green is a retired university professor and administrator. He has published five chapbooks of poetry, and individual poems have appeared in literary journals in Ireland, the UK, and the USA. James is a member of Last Stanza Poetry Association. His website can be found at www.jamesgreenpoetry.net. His latest chapbook is 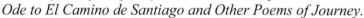 *Ode to El Camino de Santiago and Other Poems of Journey.*

Will Griffith is a poet from Cornwall who teaches philosophy in a Secondary School. He has had work published online and in print and is working on his first collection.

John D. Groppe, Professor Emeritus at Saint Joseph's College,  Rensselaer, IN, has published in *Tipton Poetry Journal, Flying Island, From the Edge of the Prairie, Christianity Today, The National Catholic Reporter,* and other journals. His poem "A Prophet Came to Town" was nominated for a Pushcart Prize (2013). His poem "Sudden Death" won honorable mention in Embers poetry contest (1984). His poetry collection *The Raid of the Grackles and Other Poems* (Iroquois River Press) was published in 2016. He is listed on the Indiana Bicentennial Literary Map 200 Years: 200 Writers.

Chris Hasara is a father of four and husband of one in Northern Indiana. He studied creative writing at Western Kentucky University and has applied that education to a successful career as a truck driver and farmer. His words have appeared in *From the Edge of the Prairie,* recent volumes of *The Last Stanza Poetry Journal,* and volume 6 of the Poetry Society of Indiana book *Ink to Paper.*

Shayla Hawkins is a Detroit native, poet, and writer whose works have been in *Calabash, tongues of the ocean, The Taj Mahal Review,* and *Poets & Writers Magazine,* among other publications. Ms. Hawkins has been a featured reader at the Geraldine R. Dodge Poetry Festival and the Library of Congress. She  also is a past winner of The Caribbean Writer's Canute A. Brodhurst Prize in Short Fiction. Her first book, *Carambola,* was published in 2012 by David Robert Books. The manuscript for her second book of poems, *Exquisite by September,* was runner-up for the 2020 Cave Canem Northwestern University Press Poetry Prize. Ms. Hawkins has also published poems in several anthologies, including *Mona Poetica, Chopin with Cherries, Delirious: A Poetic Celebration of Prince,* and *Joys of the Table: An Anthology of Culinary Verse.* She lives in Michigan.

Elizabeth Hill is a retired Administrative Law Judge who decided suits between learning disabled children and their school systems. She lives in Harlem, NYC with her husband and two irascible cats. She grew up in New Hampshire and on Cape Cod. Her poetry has been/is soon to be published in *34th Parallel Magazine, Blue Lake Review*, and *I-70 Review,* among other journals.

John R. Hinton is an Indiana poet and writer. His writing is inspired by  our daily human interactions and the accompanying emotions: love, hate, indifference, passion. His words explore who we are, how we behave. Sometimes eloquent, other times gritty, these words seek to reveal the joy and pain of living this beautiful human existence. He is the author of two poetry collections: *Blackbird Songs* and *Held.* John is the Vice President of the Poetry Society of Indiana and a member of Last Stanza Poetry Association.

Kaela Hinton is an aspiring poet from Indiana writing about deep emotions that come from living life and experiencing the world around her. She currently works with children who are on the autism spectrum, and she also frequently dabbles in the culinary field.

Mary Hinton, inspired by her poet husband John, has recently been exploring the art of haiku. She lives in Indiana with her husband, three large dogs, and her ball python, Sarin.

Liza Hyatt is a poet whose books include *Once, There Was a Canal* (Chatter House Press, 2017), *The Mother Poems* (Chatter House Press, 2014), *Under My Skin,* (WordTech Editions, 2012), *Seasons of the Star Planted Garden* (Stonework Press, 1999), and *Stories Made of World* (Finishing Line Press, 2013). She received an Individual Arts Project Grant from the Indiana Arts Commission to research Irish immigrant family history in 19th century Indiana. This research led to the poems in *Once, There Was a Canal.* She is a 2017 recipient of the Creative Renewal Arts Fellowship from the Indianapolis Arts Council. Liza is an art therapist at IU Health Charis Center for Eating Disorders. She is an adjunct professor  in the Art Therapy Master's program at St. Mary of the Woods College.

She also provides dreamwork and spiritual guidance using expressive arts and inter-spiritual practices. Her blog Soulfaring: Imagination's Homing Journey through Art, Poetry and Dreams can be found at www.lizahyatt.com

Colin James has published two chapbooks of poetry: *Dreams of the Really Annoying* from Writing Knights Press and *A Thoroughness Not Deprived of Absurdity* from Piski's Porch Press. His book of poems, *Resisting Probability,* was published by Sagging Meniscus Press. Formally from the UK, he now lives in Massachusetts.

Michael Lee Johnson lived ten years in Canada during the Vietnam era. Today he is a poet in the greater Chicagoland area. Michael Lee Johnson is an internationally published poet in 43 countries, has several published poetry books, and was nominated for four Pushcart Prize awards and five Best of the Net recognitions. He is editor-in-chief of three poetry anthologies, all available on Amazon, and has several poetry books and chapbooks. Over five hundred of his poems have been published, and he is the administrator of six Facebook poetry groups. Member of the Illinois State Poetry Society.

LeAnn Jones is a retired social worker who enjoys reading and writing poetry. She has four granddaughters who take up her time and devotion. She likes to travel, enjoys any kind of art, dances, and practices yoga. LeAnn is a member of Last Stanza Poetry Association.

Jenny Kalahar is the editor and publisher of *Last Stanza Poetry Journal.* She is the founding leader of Last Stanza Poetry Association in  Elwood, Indiana. Jenny and her husband, poet Patrick, are used and rare booksellers. She was the humor columnist for *Tails Magazine* for several years and the treasurer for Poetry Society of Indiana. Author of fourteen books, she was twice nominated for a Pushcart Prize and once for Best of the Net. Her poems have been published in *Tipton Poetry Journal, Indiana Voice Journal, Trillium, Polk Street Review, Flying Island,* and in several anthologies and newspapers. Her works can be found on poemhunter.com and *INverse,* Indiana's poetry archive. Through Stackfreed Press, she has published books for numerous authors. Contact her at laststanza@outlook.com

Patrick Kalahar is a used and rare bookseller with his wife, Jenny, and a book conservationist. He is a veteran, world traveler, avid reader, and book collector. He is a member of Last Stanza Poetry Association. His poems have been published in *Tipton Poetry Journal, Flying Island, Rail Lines, The Moon and Humans, Polk Street Review, Northwest Indiana Literary Journal,* and *A Disconsolate Planet.* Patrick can be seen as an interviewee in the Emmy-winning documentary *James Whitcomb Riley: Hoosier Poet,* and he gives costumed and scholarly readings as Edgar Allan Poe.

Chuck Kellum began writing poetry while a senior in college studying engineering and wrote about 120 poems over a dozen years before getting married, but then was too busy after that with work and family. Poetry writing resumed in 2009 after he was no longer working full time and the youngest child was off to college. He currently serves as both Treasurer and Contest Director of the Poetry Society of Indiana.

Joseph Kerschbaum's most recent publications include *Mirror Box* (Main St Rag Press, 2020) and *Distant Shore of a Split Second* (Louisiana Literature Press, 2018). Joseph has been awarded grants from the National Endowment for the Arts and the Indiana Arts Commission. His work has appeared in journals such as *Hamilton Stone Review, Panoply, Flying Island, Ponder Review, Main St. Rag, The Inflectionist Review, Last Stanza Poetry Journal,* and *Black Coffee Review.* Joseph lives in Bloomington, Indiana with his family.

Norbert Krapf, former Indiana Poet Laureate, loves gardening, playing with his Colombian-German-American grandson Peyton, seven, and learning how to grow through the writing of poetry and prose memoirs. His fifteenth poetry collection, *Spirit Sister Dance,* and his *Homecomings: A Writer's Memoir,* will be published this year. His play *Catholic Boy Blues*, an adaptation of his poetry collection of the same title, was given a workshop production of five performances in the Indy Eleven Theatre of Indy Fringe. He has released a poetry and jazz CD with pianist-composer Monika Herzig and has performed poetry and blues with Gordon Bonham.

Judith A. Lawrence is a painter/writer of fiction/memoir/poetry. Originally from Philadelphia, PA, she now resides in Florida. She has published five chapbooks of poems, written a volume of short stories, and a memoir. She is currently working on a murder/mystery novel and a book of short poems with her watercolors. Art/Poems/Short Stories were recently published in *The Linnets Wings, Songs of Eretz, Sweetycat Press,* and *Short Story Town.*

Deborah Zarka Miller holds an MFA in writing and teaches composition, creative writing, and literature at Anderson University, a small liberal arts school in central Indiana. In addition to teaching, she has served as lead grant writer and project manager for several large initiatives funded by Lilly Endowment and is co-director of the university's Honors Program. She was the editor for *The Desk as Altar: The Centennial History of Anderson University*, published in 2016. Her publications  include *A Star for Robbins Chapel*, a young adult novella published in 2010 by Chinaberry House and multiple articles on pedagogy in higher education, all of which appeared in *Faculty Focus.* She also contributed an essay to *Home Again: Essays and Memoirs from Indiana,* published in 2006 by the Indiana Historical Society Press.

Lylanne Musselman is an award-winning poet, playwright, and visual artist. Her work has appeared in *Tipton Poetry Journal, Flying Island, Last Stanza Poetry Journal,* and *The Ekphrastic Review,* among many others, in addition to many anthologies.  She is author of six chapbooks, and her seventh, *Staring Dementia in the Face,* is forthcoming from Finishing Line Press. Musselman is author of the full-length poetry collection, *It's Not Love, Unfortunately* (Chatter House Press, 2018). A four-time Pushcart Prize nominee, her poems are included in the INverse Poetry Archive, a collection of Hoosier poets housed at the Indiana State Library.

Matt Nagin's poetry has been published in *The Antigonish Review, Oxford Magazine, Grain Magazine,* and *Arsenic Lobster*. His work is also included in the anthologies *New York's Best Emerging Poets 2019* and *Poetry in the Time of Coronavirus*. One poem, "If We are Doomed," won *the 2018 Spirit First Editor's Choice Award*. He has published three books of poetry, his latest being *Notes from the Bonfire*. More info at mattnagin.com

James B. Nicola's poems have appeared in the *Antioch, Southwest,* and *Atlanta Reviews; Rattle;* and *Barrow Street*. His full-length collections (2014-21) are *Manhattan Plaza, Stage to Page, Wind in the Cave, Out of Nothing, Quickening,* and *Fires of Heaven*. His nonfiction book *Playing the Audience* won a *Choice* award. His poetry has received a Dana Literary Award, two *Willow Review* awards, *Storyteller's* People's Choice award, and eight Pushcart nominations—for which he feels both stunned and grateful.

James Nolan's latest book of poetry is *Nasty Water: Collected New Orleans Poems* (University of Louisiana at Lafayette Press, 2018). Previous collections are *Why I Live in the Forest, What Moves Is Not the Wind,* and *Drunk on Salt*, and his translations include volumes of Neruda and Gil de Biedma. His *Flight Risk* won the 2018 Next-Generation Indie Book Award for Best Memoir. The three books of his fiction have been awarded a Faulkner-Wisdom Gold Medal, an Independent Publishers Book Award, and a Next-Generation Indie Book Award. The recipient of an NEA and two Fulbright fellowships, he has taught at universities in San Francisco, Florida, Barcelona, Madrid, Beijing, as well as in his native New Orleans. www.pw.org/directory/writers/james_nolan

Kathy O'Fallon's poems and short stories have been published in numerous literary journals, magazines, anthologies, such as *RATTLE, Salt Marsh Poetry Press, Sou'wester,* etc., along with three chapbooks. She was a finalist for The Backwater's Prize for her manuscript, *Listening to Tchaikovsky,* and for *Adfinitas* with Inlandia. O'Fallon is a psychologist working in Carlsbad, CA.

 **Regina O'Melveny** is a writer and artist whose award-winning poetry and prose have been anthologized and widely published in *The Bellingham Review, The Sun, West Marin Review, Solo, Barrow Street,* and elsewhere. Her long poem, *Fireflies,* won the Conflux Press Poetry Award and was published as an artist's book designed by Tania Baban. She has published three chapbooks, *Secret, New,* and most recently, *other gods,* which won a prize from the Munster International Literary Centre in Cork, Ireland. Her manuscript *Blue Wolves,* won the Bright Hill Press poetry book award. Sheila-Na-Gig Editions released *The Shape of Emptiness,* her second full-length poetry book. Her novel, *The Book of Madness and Cures,* published by Little, Brown and Company, was listed as one of the six best historical novels of the year 2012 by NPR. She has taught writing at Marymount California University, the Palos Verdes Art Center, and the South Coast Botanic Gardens. She lives in Rancho Palos Verdes with her husband.

E. Martin Pedersen, originally from San Francisco, has lived for over forty years in eastern Sicily, where he taught English at the local university. His poetry appeared most recently in *Ginosko, Metaworker, Triggerfish, Unlikely Stories Mark V,* and *Grey Sparrow Review,* among others. Martin is an alumnus of the Community of Writers. He has published two collections of haiku, *Bitter Pills* and *Smart Pills,* and a chapbook, *Exile's Choice,* from Kelsay Books. A  full collection, *Method & Madness,* is forthcoming from Odyssey Press. Martin blogs at: https://emartinpedersenwriter.blogspot.com

Rosanne Megenity Peters believes poems are messengers sent by the soul to nourish, instruct, and reveal us. Her poems usually arrive in the middle of the night and rattle about the room until she yields to the impulse to write.

Nancy Kay Peterson's poetry has appeared in print and online in numerous publications, most recently in *Dash Literary Journal, Her Words, Last Stanza Poetry Journal, One Sentence Poems, Spank the Carp, Steam Ticket: A Third Coast Review, Tipton Poetry Journal* and *Three Line Poetry.* From 2004-2009, she co-edited and co-published *Main Channel Voices: A Dam Fine Literary Magazine* (Winona, MN). Finishing Line Press published her two poetry chapbooks, *Belated*

Remembrance (2010) and *Selling the Family* (2021). For more information, seewww.nancykaypeterson.com.

Samuel Prestridge lives in Athens, Georgia. He has been published in *Literary Imagination, Style, The Arkansas Review, As It Ought To Be, Poetry Quarterly, Appalachian Quarterly, Paideuma, The Lullwater Review, Poem,* and *The Southern Humanities Review.* "I write poetry," he says, "because there are matters that cannot be directly stated, but that are essential to the survival of whatever soul we can still have. Also, I'm no good at  interpretive dance, which is the only other option that's occurred to me." He is a post-aspirational man whose first book, *A Pebble's Worth of Riot, A Dog's Job of Work,* seeks publication.

Carlos Reyes's recent poetry: *Osage Elegy* (2021), *The Ebbing Tide* (2021), *Lament for Us All* (2021), *Sea Smoke to Ashes* (2020), *Along the Flaggy Shore,* (2018), *Wrestling the Mistral* (2022). Translations: *Poemas de amor y locura/Poems of Love and Madness* (2013). *The Keys to the Cottage, Stories from the West of Ireland* (2015). He lives in Portland, Oregon.

Stephen R. Roberts collects books, geodes, gargoyles, poetic lariats, and various other objects of interest to enhance his basic perceptions of a chaotic planet that pays little attention to him, as far as he knows. He has been published in *Briar Cliff Review, Borderlands, Slant, Willow Springs, Karamu, Water-Stone, Yalobusha Review,* and numerous others. His full-length collection, *Almost Music from Between Places,* is from Chatter House Press.

Kit Rohrbach's most recent volume of poetry is *Unless It's Winter* (Zumbro River Press). She lives with four cats in southern Minnesota.

Brenda Ross grew up on the outskirts of Clear Lake, Iowa, where she wrote for the *Mirror-Reporter* and *The Resorter*. She studied

Interpersonal Communication at the University of Northern Iowa, followed by Information Science & Learning Technologies at the University of Missouri-Columbia. Brenda now lives in the Quad Cities, where the Mississippi River runs east to west. When she isn't snuggling her husband and two sons, she is working as a librarian at the Davenport Public Library. Brenda enjoys (in alphabetical order) dancing, gardening, and hiking the trails near her home.

Qassim Saudi has published several volumes of poetry as well as children's books. He manages a publishing house for children's literature in Baghdad, where he was born in 1969.

Poet, writer, and lifelong student of the Bible, **Mary Harwell Sayler** writes in all genres for Christian, educational, and indie publishers. After collecting actual prayers from God's word into *the Book of Bible Prayers,* she did additional research for *Kneeling on the Promises of God.* Her book, *A Gathering of Poems,* collects many of her poems previously published in magazines, anthologies, or journals.

Mary Sexson is author of the award-winning book, *103 in the Light, Selected Poems 1996-2000 (*Restoration Press*),* and co-author of *Company of Women, New and Selected Poems* (Chatter House Press). Her poetry has appeared in *Tipton Poetry Journal, Laureate, Literary Journal of Arts for Lawrence, Hoosier Lit, Flying Island, New Verse News*, and *Last Stanza Poetry Journal,* among

others. Sexson's poems are also included in various anthologies. She has recent work in the anthology *Reflections on Little Eagle Creek,* in *Anti-Heroin Chic* (October 2021), and in Issue #7 *Last Stanza Poetry Journal. Anti-Heroin Chic* has just published one of Sexson's poems in its February 2022 online edition. Her work is part of INverse Poetry Archives for Hoosier Poets.

A lifelong Southern Californian, **Joanne Sharp** holds a BA in Art and Design from UCLA, class of 1961. She is a visual artist with strong interests in music, literature, textiles, and costume. Joanne and her late husband, an artist/partner, designed and built their home in Del Mar, California where she still resides. A memoir workshop in 2014 sparked renewed interest in poetry, which she has written on and off since childhood and  is now her primary creative focus. Joanne's poetry has appeared in the *San Diego Poetry Annual, Summations Art and Poetry, California Quarterly,* and *Writers Resist.*

Robert Simon holds the title of Professor of Spanish and Portuguese at Kennesaw State University. Along with his numerous academic publications, he has also published ten collections of poetry, including *Ode to Friendship* (2021), *The Bridge* (2019), and *The Musician* (2017), along with poems in various journals in India, Portugal, and the United States. He enjoys reading, running, spending time with his daughter, and playing the oboe.

Paul Smith is a civil engineer who has worked in the construction business for many years. He has traveled all over and met lots of people. Some have enriched his life. Others gave him the material writers need, the kind of things you just can't make up. He likes writing poetry and fiction. He also likes Newcastle Brown Ale. If you see him, buy him one. His poetry and fiction have been published in *Convergence, Missouri Review, Literary Orphans,* and other literary magazines.

Michael E. Strosahl was born and raised in Moline, Illinois, just blocks from the Mississippi River. He has written poetry since youth. After moving to Tipton, Indiana, he participated in a poetry reading on a dare at the Barnes & Noble in Westfield, Indiana, 2001. He then became active in the Indiana poetry scene, becoming involved in what is now known as the Poetry Society of Indiana. He traveled the state in search of small groups that met in living rooms, libraries, and coffee houses, and he started groups in communities where he found  none. He served the PSI as Membership Chair and eventually as President. In 2018, he relocated to Jefferson City, MO, beginning his search anew for kindred spirits to inspire and draw energy from. He currently co-hosts a monthly critique group in the capital city and is a member of Last Stanza Poetry Association.

Connie S. Tettenborn, now living near San Francisco, began writing poetry as a 9-year-old in Ohio and has since never completely stopped, even while obtaining her PhD in Oncology from the University of Wisconsin-Madison and then working at various biotech companies. A transition to scientific editing yielded more time to focus on her poetry, which also includes visual and mathematical poetry created using watercolor or digital media. Her works have appeared in *The Deronda Review* and *California Quarterly*, as well as various online venues such as *Otoliths* and *The Piker Press*.

David Vancil is retired from the faculty of Indiana State University. His work has appeared in small periodicals, critical reviews, and a few anthologies. As well, he is the author of four poetry collections. *Expiation: War and Its Discontents*, a collection of military poems centered on family service and his own time in the U.S. Army, will be published by Angelina River Press in 2022. He is at work on a collection of new and selected poems, which he hopes to publish no later than 2023. David lives with his wife, three cats, and a dog.

Rp Verlaine lives in New York City. He has an MFA in creative writing from City College. He taught in New York Public schools for many years. His first volume of poetry, *Damaged by Dames & Drinking,* was published in 2017, and another, *Femme Fatales Movie Starlets & Rockers,* in 2018. A set of three ebooks titled *Lies from the Autobiography, vol. 1-3,* were published from 2018 to 2020. His newest book, *Imagined Indecencies,* came out in 2022.

Melody Wang currently resides in sunny Southern California with her dear husband and wishes it were autumn all year 'round. Her debut collection of poetry, *Night-blooming Cereus*, was released in 2021 with Alien Buddha Press. She can be found on Twitter @MelodyOfMusings or at her website https://linktr.ee/MelodyOfMusings

Carrie Weinberger lives, writes, and keeps tethered to the green world in her Carlsbad, California garden. She is a former teacher of English Literature, and her study of painting at Rhode Island School of Design merges in her poetry a love of sensory words and images. Her poems have most recently appeared in the *California Poetry Quarterly*, *East on Central*, and *Raven's Perch*.

J. T. Whitehead earned a law degree from Indiana University, Bloomington and a master's degree in philosophy from Purdue. Whitehead was Editor in Chief of *So It Goes: The Literary Journal of the Kurt Vonnegut Memorial Library*, briefly, for issues 1, 2, 3, 4, and 6. He is a *Pushcart Prize*-nominated short story author, a *Pushcart Prize*-nominated poet, and was winner of the *Margaret Randall Poetry Prize* in 2015 (published in *Mas Tequila Review*). Whitehead's poetry has appeared in over 100 publications, including *The Lilliput Review*, *Slipstream*, *Left Curve*, *The Broadkill Review*, *The Blue Collar Review*, *Home Planet News*, *The Iconoclast*, *Poetry Hotel*, *Book XI*, and *Gargoyle*. His book *The Table of the Elements* was nominated for the *National Book Award* in 2015. Whitehead lives in Indianapolis with his two sons, Daniel and Joseph.

Matthew Whybrew is an Indiana-based writer and mental health clinician. He grew up on a farm in rural north-central Indiana where he spent much of his time in nature and its beauty. His experiences in the mental health field as well as his humble upbringing have colored his writing and other artistic endeavors. Matthew often draws from his own struggles with mental health to create relatable pieces that may be helpful to others. His mission is to bring meaningful and wholesome life to those with whom he interacts.

Robin Wright lives in Southern Indiana. Her work has appeared in *One Art*, *Young Ravens Literary Review*, *Olney Magazine*, *As it Ought to Be*, *Rat's Ass Review*, *Sledgehammer Lit*, *Muddy River Poetry Review*, *Sanctuary*, and others. She is a Pushcart Prize nominee, and her first chapbook, *Ready or Not*, was published by Finishing Line Press in October of 2020.

RM Yager is a retired nurse/teacher/photographer whose topics are marginalized, at risk populations. Poetry is her vehicle to deliver words most people find unspeakable. She hopes to offer inclusion and wants to stop you in your tracks with controversial humor/tragedy within family and relationships, but she also loves whimsy, humor, and nature. She has been published in the US and internationally.

Bill Yarrow, Professor of English at Joliet Junior College, is the author of eleven books of poetry including *Blasphemer, The Vig of Love*, and, most recently, *Accelerant*. His poems have been published in *Poetry International, FRiGG, Gargoyle, PANK, Confrontation, Contrary, Diagram, Thrush, Chiron Review, RHINO, Into the Void, FIVE: 2:ONE*, and many other journals. He has been nominated eight times for a Pushcart Prize.

Hiromi Yoshida is the author of three poetry chapbooks, *Icarus Burning, Epicanthus*, and *Icarus Redux*. Her work has been nominated for the Pushcart Prize, Best of the Net, the Wilder Poetry Book Prize, the New Women's Voices Poetry Prize, and the Gerald Cable Book Award. She is the diversity consultant for the Writers Guild at Bloomington; a poetry instructor at the Indiana Writers Center; and a poetry reader for *Flying Island Journal* and *Plath Profiles*.

Judy Young is a lifelong Elwood, Indiana poet and member of Last Stanza Poetry Association, the Poetry Society of Indiana, and the National Federation of State Poetry Societies. She is married with five children, nine grandbabies, and seven great-grandchildren. She is the author of *Wild Wood* and *Moonset,* and has been published in *Tipton Poetry Journal, Indiana Voice Journal,* and in several  anthologies and other journals. She is a nature advocate and tree enthusiast.

Made in the USA
Middletown, DE
17 April 2022